W9-BBW-800

**Governor Zell Miller's
Reading Initiative**

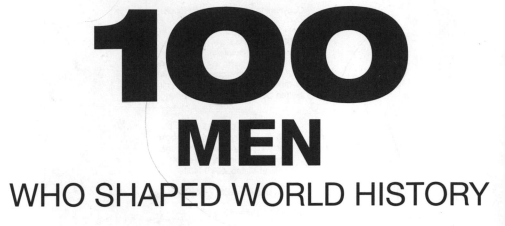

100
MEN
WHO SHAPED WORLD HISTORY

Bill Yenne

A Bluewood Book
(1994)

This edition was produced and published in 1994 by Bluewood Books A division of The Siyeh Group, Inc., 38 South B Street, Suite 202 San Mateo, CA 94401

ISBN 0-912517-05-0

Printed in USA

Designed and captioned by Tom Debolski

Cover illustration by Vadim Vahrameev

Key to front cover illustration:
1. Napoleon Bonaparte
2. Albert Einstein
3. John F. Kennedy
4. Martin Luther King, Jr.
5. Leonardo da Vinci
6. Thomas Alva Edison
7. Winston Churchill
8. Franklin D. Roosevelt
9. Josef Stalin
10. Galileo Galilei

About the Author:

Bill Yenne is a San Francisco-based writer and radio commentator. He is the author of more than 20 books on historical topics, including *100 Events That Shaped World History* and *100 Inventions That Shaped World History*, also in this series, which WTAE-Radio (Pittsburgh) called "compelling" and KGO-Radio (San Francisco) called "most fascinating." The Texas USA Network said of these books, "If you're a student of history, you're going to *want* these books. If you're not a student of history, your're going to *need* these books." Among his recent books are *The World's Worst Aircraft*, which KABC-Radio (Los Angeles) called "amazing" and CJCA-Radio (Edmonton) called "a real masterpiece" and *Black '41, The West Point Class of 1941* and the *American Triumph in World War II*, which WOAI-Radio (San Antonio) called "the epitome of the best war story you'll ever hear."

Mr. Yenne's other works include a series of books on America's great planemakers, which includes *Boeing: Planemaker to the World* (with Robert Redding); *Lockheed: Reaching for the Stars; McDonnell Douglas: A Tale of Two Giants* and *Rockwell: The Heritage of North American.*

Mr. Yenne has also written *The History of the US Air Force, The History of Northwest Airlines;* and *Superfortress: The B-29* and *American Airpower* (with General Curtis E. LeMay). His first novel, an action adventure story set against a backdrop of modern aviation developments, was published in 1994.

TABLE OF CONTENTS

INTRODUCTION 7
1. PHARAOH MENES 8
c. 3100 BC
2. HAMMURABI 9
1792-1750 BC
3. MOSES 10
1300-c. 1220 BC
4. HOMER 11
c. 850 BC
5. LAO TSU (LAO TSE) 12
604-531 BC
6. BUDDHA
(SIDDHARTHA GAUTAMA) 13
563-483 BC
7. CYRUS THE GREAT 14
c. 558-528 BC
8. CONFUCIUS (KUNG FU-TSU) 15
551-479 BC
9. XERXES I 16
519-465 BC
10. PERICLES 17
500-429 BC
11. HERODOTUS 18
c. 485-425 BC
12. SOCRATES 19
469-399 BC
13. HIPPOCRATES 20
460-375 BC

14. PLATO 21
427-347 BC
15. ARISTOTLE 22
384-322 BC
16. ALEXANDER THE GREAT 23
356-323 BC
17. ASOKA 24
?-232 BC
18. ARCHIMEDES 25
287-212 BC
19. SHIH HUANG TI 26
259-210 BC
20. GAIUS JULIUS CAESAR 27
102-44 BC
21. CAESAR AUGUSTUS
(OCTAVIAN) 28
63 BC-14 AD
22. JESUS CHRIST 29
4 BC-29 AD
23. ST. PAUL (SAUL OF TARSUS) 30
5-67 AD
24 CONSTANTINE 31
280-337 AD
25. ST. AUGUSTINE 32
354-430 AD
26. MOHAMMED 33
570-632 AD

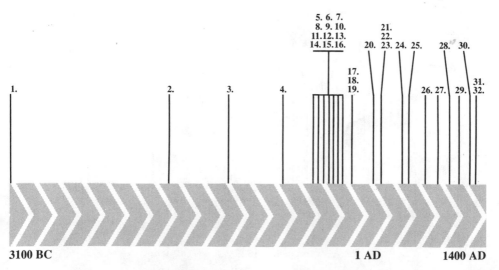

5. 6. 7.
8. 9. 10.   21.
11.12.13.   22.
14.15.16.   20. 23. 24. 25.   28. 30.

17.
18.   31.
1.   2.   3.   4.   19.   26. 27. 29. 32.

3100 BC   1 AD   1400 AD

27. CHARLEMAGNE *34*
    742-814 AD

28. OTTO I *35*
    912-973 AD

29. WILLIAM THE CONQUEROR *36*
    1027-1087

30. GENGHIS KHAN (TEMUJIN) *37*
    1167-1227

31. ST. THOMAS AQUINAS *38*
    1225-1274

32. MARCO POLO *39*
    1254?-1324

33. JOHANN GUTENBERG *40*
    1400-1468

34. CHRISTOPHER COLUMBUS *41*
    1451-1506

35. LEONARDO DA VINCI *42*
    1452-1519

36. DESIDERIUS ERASMUS *43*
    1466-1536

37. NICHOLAS COPERNICUS
    (KOPERNICK) *44*
    1473-1543

38. MICHAELANGELO
    BUONARROTI *45*
    1475-1564

39. FERDINAND MAGELLAN *46*
    1480-1521

40. MARTIN LUTHER *47*
    1483-1546

41. HENRY VIII *48*
    1491-1547

42. GALILEO GALILEI *49*
    1564-1642

43. WILLIAM SHAKESPEARE *50*
    1564-1616

44. OLIVER CROMWELL *51*
    1599-1658

45. SIR ISAAC NEWTON *52*
    1642-1727

46. JOHANN SEBASTIAN BACH *53*
    1685-1750

47. VOLTAIRE
    (FRANCOIS MARIE AROUET) *54*
    1694-1778

48. BENJAMIN FRANKLIN *55*
    1706-1790

49. FREDERICK II (THE GREAT) *56*
    1712-1786

50. JAMES COOK *57*
    1728-1779

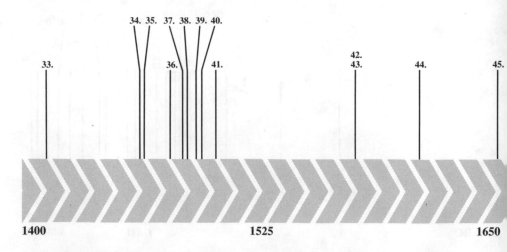

34. 35. 37. 38. 39. 40.

33. 36. 41. 42. 43. 44. 45.

1400 1525 1650

51.	GEORGE WASHINGTON *58* 1732-1799	**64.**	WILLIAM EWART GLADSTONE *72* 1809-1898
52.	THOMAS JEFFERSON *59* 1743-1826	**65.**	CHARLES DICKENS 73 1812-1870
53.	WOLFGANG AMADEUS MOZART *60* 1756-1791	**66.**	OTTO EDUARD LEOPOLD VON BISMARCK *74* 1815-1898
54.	LUDWIG VON BEETHOVEN *61* 1770-1827	**67.**	JULES VERNE *75* 1829-1905
55.	NAPOLEON BONAPARTE *62* 1769-1821	**68.**	CHIEF SITTING BUFFALO BULL (TATANKYA IYOTAKE) *76*
56-57.	WILLIAM CLARK 1770-1838 *64* and MERRIWETHER LEWIS 1774-1809	**69.**	1834-1890 MARK TWAIN (SAMUEL CLEMENS) *77*
58.	SIMÓN BOLÍVAR *65* 1783-1830	**70.**	1835-1910 THOMAS ALVA EDISON *78*
59.	SAMUEL MORSE *66* 1791-1872	**71.**	1847-1931 ALEXANDER GRAHAM BELL *80*
60.	BENJAMIN DISRAELI *67* 1804-1881	**72.**	1847-1922 MUTSUHITO (MEIJI) *81*
61.	GIUSEPPE GARIBALDI *68* 1808-1882	**73.**	1852-1912 SIGMUND FREUD *82*
62.	CHARLES DARWIN *69* 1809-1882	**74.**	1856-1939 THEODORE ROOSEVELT *83*
63.	ABRAHAM LINCOLN *70* 1809-1865	**75.**	1858-1919 HENRY FORD *84* 1863-1947

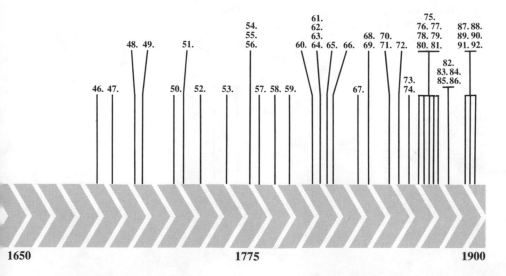

1650   1775   1900

76-77. WILBUR WRIGHT 1867-1912 *85*
and ORVILLE WRIGHT 1871-1948

78. MOHANDAS KARAMCHAND
"MAHATMA" GANDHI *86*
1869-1948

79. NIKOLAI LENIN
(VLADIMIR ILYICH ULIANOV) *87*
1870-1924

80. SIR WINSTON CHURCHILL *88*
1874-1965

81. GUGILELMO MARCONI *89*
1874-1937

82. ALBERT EINSTEIN *90*
1879-1955

83. JOSEF STALIN
(JOSEF DJUGASHVILI) *91*
1879-1953

84. DOUGLAS MACARTHUR *92*
1880-1964

85. PABLO PICASSO *93*
1881-1973

86. FRANKLIN DELANO
ROOSEVELT *94*
1882-1945

87. CHARLES SPENCER
"CHARLIE" CHAPLIN *96*
1889-1977

88. ADOLF HITLER *97*
1889-1945

89. CHARLES ANDRE MARIE
JOSEPH DE GAULLE *98*
1890-1970

90. DWIGHT DAVID EISENHOWER *99*
1890-1969

91. MAO TSE-TUNG
(MAO ZEDONG) *100*
1893-1976

92. GEORGE HERMAN
"BABE" RUTH *101*
1895-1948

93. WERNHER VON BRAUN *102*
1912-1977

94. JOHN FITZGERALD KENNEDY *103*
1917-1963

95. DR. MARTIN LUTHER
KING, JR. *104*
1929-1968

96. MIKHAIL SERGEYEVICH
GORBACHEV *105*
b. 1931

97. STEPHEN WILLIAM HAWKING *106*
b. 1942

98-99. STEPHEN WOZNIAK b. 1950 *107*
and STEVEN PAUL JOBS b. 1955

100. WILLIAM HENRY GATES *108*
b. 1955

TRIVIA QUIZ & GAMES *109*

INDEX *110*

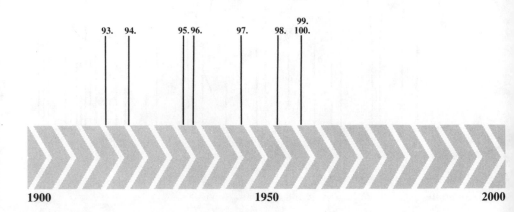

93. 94. 95. 96. 97. 98. 99. 100.

1900   1950   2000

6

INTRODUCTION

History is populated with tens of thousands of people who have made a significant difference. However, among these are figures who have risen as true beacons of greatness—for either good or ill—on the highways of history. This book, and the companion volume, *100 Women Who Shaped World History,* seeks to provide capsule views of these exceptional people.

Whatever their accomplishments, we can learn from them, for they have truly effected our lives in both subtle and profound ways. There have been great leaders and prophets, just as there have been sadistic tyrants and charlatans. Many of the prominent people in history have been hated by some and praised by others—it's often a matter of perspective. Then, too, it is often a matter of timing. In his own time, **Christopher Columbus** was celebrated for opening up navigation to unknown lands, but he also spent time in jail. At the end of the nineteenth century, he was seen as a heroic explorer. However, by the close of the twentieth century, he had come to be viewed more as a villain.

To select a mere 100 men from the multitude of important historical figures, we have attempted to gather a variety of men from diverse backgrounds.

There are the founders of the world's major religions: **Jesus Christ, Mohammed, Buddha** and **Confucius**.

There are heroic conquerors: **Alexander the Great, Julius Caesar** and **Napoleon Bonaparte.**

There are compelling artists: **Leonardo da Vinci, Wolfgang Amadeus Mozart** and **William Shakespeare**.

There are pioneering scientists: **Archimedes, Sir Isaac Newton, Albert Einstein** and **Steven Hawking**.

There are notable statesmen: **George Washington, Winston Churchill** and **Mikhail Gorbachev.**

Then, too, there are monumental villains: **Genghis Khan, Adolf Hitler** and **Josef Stalin.**

What all these men have in common is that they significantly impacted the course of history by their presence on the world stage at a particular moment in time. These men, like the women in our companion volume, distinguished themselves as role models, attaining what others had sought to do, and they earned the respect, envy or hatred of the world community for their accomplishments. We can learn much by studying the source and scope of their fame—or infamy—and the way their actions and accomplishments altered the course of world events.

Josef Stalin, Franklin D. Roosevelt and Winston Churchill.

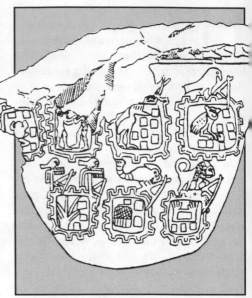

The emergence of a man capable of shaping world history was dependent on the evolution of a setting where such an event was possible. In order for a man to play such a role, there had to be a stage. The stage upon which **Menes** stepped was the fertile lower Nile in what is now Egypt.

Human society evolved from small bands to tribes and eventually into city-states that were self-governing units. Gradually, the influence of a more powerful city-state would expand and incorporate surrounding villages. By 3300 BC, the towns along the Nile River had formed into the two kingdoms of Upper Egypt **(The White Crown)** and Lower Egypt **(The Red Crown)**. In 3100 BC, Menes, who wore the red crown of lower Egypt, unified the two kingdoms into the world's first empire.

Menes created a political entity the likes of which had never before existed. Organized societies had grown larger through the mergers of smaller entities for several thousand years, but when Menes created a united Egypt, his new empire reached a sort of critical mass. Suddenly, Egypt was more than just the sum of its parts, more than just a red crown and a white crown on the head of the same man. These two parts became melded into a single, cosmopolitan unit, the world's first empire, a political entity that would permit—for the first time in history—the development of a broad-based socioeconomic system.

It probably would have happened elsewhere eventually, but it happened in Egypt first. As a result, Egypt led the world for the next several centuries. We'll never know whether Menes envisioned what came to pass, but the fact that his empire endured does speak to his genius as a political leader. He ruled from the ancient city

It was during the reign of Pharaoh Menes that the first hieroglyphic alphabet is believed to have been developed.

of Thinis near Abydos and under his reign the first hieroglyphic alphabet is believed to have been adopted.

Under the rule of Menes and his successors, which lasted for 2500 years, Egypt developed a culture more complex than any before it. Individual cities no longer had to be self-sufficient and they so became interdependent. At the center of this society, the court of the pharaohs developed great wealth and power—both political and religious. A pharaoh was considered more than a king and came to be worshipped as a god. Magnificent cities and large-scale engineering projects were undertaken.

The empire of the pharaohs eventually collapsed, superseded and dominated by new empires, but the legacy of the pharaohs, ranging from science to architecture, is still remembered and respected as one of the true milestones in human civilization.

2. HAMMURABI
1792-1750 BC

Hammurabi was the sixth king of Babylon's first dynasty and he may have been **"Amraphel,"** the king of Shinoar referred to in the **Bible** (Genesis 14:1). He led his armies to defeat Akkad, Elam, Larsa, Mari and Sumer, creating the **Babylonian Empire** in much the same way that Menes had united Egypt over a thousand years before.

However, despite his great conquests, Hammurabi would be lost to the sands of time as just another mighty warlord were it not for the fact it was by his hand that the world's first true legal code was issued. Although he was a well-known and well-respected monarch remembered for putting "order and righteousness in the land," his code was little more than forgotten folklore until 1901. In that year, French archaeologists discovered among the artifacts in the ruins of ancient Babylon the **Code of Hammurabi,** carved in **cuneiform** characters on a huge stone slab.

There were 282 laws in the Code, with evidence of another 35 having been chipped off and lost. The Code identified

Hammurabi.

specific crimes and stipulated their penalties. For instance, a man who failed to repair his dike would be compelled to compensate a neighbor whose land was flooded; a priestess could be burned alive for entering a tavern without permission; a widow could inherit a portion of her husband's property equal to that inherited by their son; and a surgeon whose patient died while under the knife would lose his hand. The Code also provided for a debtor to get out of his debt by giving his wife or child to a creditor for three years.

The Code went beyond being simply a legal code by stipulating the structure of the government. And, since the king was also the chief priest, the Code governed Babylonian religious life as well. For the first time, laws were published and codified for all to see, rather than being enacted by the whim of the monarch. In this sense, Hammurabi's Code was the precursor of the legal systems under which most modern societies still function.

A letter written by Hammurabi.

3. MOSES
1300-c. 1220 BC

In the thirteenth century BC, the Hebrew people were living in Egypt where they came under official persecution. At one point, the pharaoh ordered that all male Hebrew children be put to death. The mother of **Moses,** in order to save him, placed her baby in a small reed basket and cast it adrift on the Nile River. As she intended, the child was rescued by the pharaoh's daughter and taken to live in the royal palace. When he grew to manhood, he lobbied for the emancipation of his people, which was finally, but reluctantly, granted by Pharaoh **Ramses II (1292-1225 BC).** Moses then led the Hebrew people out of Egypt, whereupon they are said to have spent 40 years wandering in the Sinai en route to their traditional homeland in what is now Israel.

In about 1250 BC, God appeared to Moses as a burning bush on the upper slopes of Mount Sinai. God gave Moses two stone tablets containing a set of laws known as the Ten Commandments. Moses took these back to his people and they adopted them as the basic moral code of Judaism. Christianity subsequently embraced the Ten Commandments and they are today among the basic beliefs of over 1.6 billion people.

Most ancient religions—such as those in Mesopotamia, Egypt, India, Greece and later Rome—were polytheistic, meaning that their followers believed in many gods and goddesses, such as a god of the Sun, a goddess of the Moon, and so on. However, the Hebrews, composed of the 12 tribes of Israel, believed in a single deity whom they called **Jehovah.** In the beginning, monotheism was a distinctly minority belief, but today it is the central doctrine for over half of the world's religiously faithful.

Moses with the stone tablets containing the Ten Commandments.

Homer was a blind poet who lived in Greece in the ninth century BC and wrote two of the most enduring epics in the history of civilization, but beyond this, few facts are known about him. He may have been a traveling minstrel or he may have been the court storyteller in one of the Greek city-states. Some even believe that he could have been an imaginary character created to explain the works that are credited to him.

At the same time in the century ascribed to Homer's lifetime, two epic poems, *The Iliad* and *The Odyssey*, appeared in Greek literature. Set against the backdrop of the **Trojan War,** they are so powerful as to have survived for centuries as literary masterpieces. *The Iliad* tells the story of **Achilles** and his quarrel with his commander **Agamemnon** over **Briseis,** a captured Trojan woman. Achilles refuses to fight the Trojans, but when his friend **Patroclus** is killed by the Trojan general, **Hector,** Achilles enters the battle to avenge his friend's death.

The Odyssey is based on the 10-year wanderings of **Odysseus** and his encounters with giants, monsters and an enchantress. When he returns home to **Ithaca,** he is forced to fend off several men at-

Homer.

tempting to woo his wife **Penelope,** who was convinced that she had become a widow. Ultimately, Odysseus regains his throne in Ithaca and is reunited with Penelope.

Other works have also been attributed to Homer, but his true legacy lies in the countless works that have been inspired by *The Iliad* and *The Odyssey*, and by the characters and mythology that he created.

Greek warriors of Homer's era training for battle.

11

5. LAO TSU (LAO TSE)
604-531 BC

Born at Keuh-jin in China, **Lao Tsu** served as the archivist to the emperors of the **Chou Dynasty**, and it was during this time that he wrote the *Tao Te Ching*, one of the oldest and most influential philosophical works to originate in the Far East. It forms the basis of **Taoism,** one of the world's great religions.

In his book, Lao Tsu describes his belief that the world order is based on the **Tao** (the *way* or path) that one follows in life. On the path, one is aware of a balance between humanity and the universe and between all of the contrasting forces within the nature of the universe and the nature of humanity. This duality and balance is summarized in the **yin** and **yang,** which literally mean the dark side and sunny side of the same hill, but which symbolize the balance of opposite elements such as dark and light, as well as male and female, weak and strong, Earth and sky, black and white or good and evil.

In following the Tao, or path, Lao Tsu theorized that one applies the idea of **Te,** which roughly translates as *virtue*. Te also adheres to the duality of yin and yang, making it possible to have both good and bad virtue, each with its own reward. In this sense, Te is like the Hindu doctrine of **karma** or the Christian idea of sin. In Hinduism, a person's reward comes after death in the cycle of reincarnation in heaven. However, in Taoism (or in physics as described in **Sir Isaac Newton's** *Third Law of Motion*) an action leads to an immediate or near-term *reaction* of equal magnitude. Lao Tsu was highly regarded in his own time and became influential to succeeding generations of theologians.

Lao Tsu.

6. BUDDHA (SIDDHARTHA GAUTAMA)
563-483 BC

Of the great organized world religions with the largest number of adherents today, two—**Judaism** and **Hinduism**—trace their roots to antiquity and as such have no specific founder. The other three—**Buddhism, Christianity** and **Islam**—were all established in historical times by specific persons. The founder of **Buddhism, Siddhartha Gautama** was born in Kapilavastu in northern India, the son of a wealthy raja named **Suddhadaha,** who was associated with the **Kshatriya,** or warrior class. Siddhartha developed an early interest in philosophy and the literature of the Vedas, the basic scriptures of Hinduism. Basically, he was interested in the pain of existence. Gradually, however, he became disenchanted with Hinduism and the suffering that he saw around him.

Siddhartha ultimately decided to develop an alternate religious philosophy that would deliver the spirit, if not the body, from earthly afflictions. When he was 29, he had a series of visions that convinced him to leave his palace and his wife and son, renounce all worldly possessions and set out in search of "truth." He visited many holy men and spent several years fasting and meditating, with his objective being to overcome all his bodily desires— including hunger—and to gain complete control over his mind.

The truth that Siddhartha sought eluded him until one night in May in about 528 BC, when, while sitting under a bo tree, he received what is known to Buddhists as Enlightenment. In this single moment, Siddhartha suddenly realized that suffering could be conquered. One of the basic doctrines of Hinduism is the cycle of reincarnation. The soul of every living thing that dies is reborn in another living thing. This cycle continues forever, with the soul gradually moving up from an insect to an animal to a human form. If a human is evil in

A giant bronze statue of Buddha.

his lifetime, he will be reborn as a lower form of life. Otherwise, he is reborn as another person. This cycle of reincarnation is infinite, but Siddhartha theorized that by following the proper path (dharma) of meditation and devotion, the soul could achieve a state of nirvana, a perfect final state not unlike the Judeo-Christian concept of heaven.

Siddhartha took the name **Buddha,** meaning "enlightened one," and went out into the world to teach his philosophy. After his death, his followers spread the Buddhist philosophy throughout Asia, finding a greater proportion of adherents in China, Japan and Southeast Asia than in India. Today, there are almost 300 million Buddhists in the world, 99.5 percent of them in Asia.

13

1. CYRUS THE GREAT
c. 558-528 BC

The great empires that have existed throughout history are important not so much for their political influence but for their cultural influence. Political control over an empire always collapses after time, but things like language, literature and customs last for centuries.

One of the earliest of the great empires and certainly one of the most important in southwest Asia and the eastern Mediterranean was the **Persian Empire** created by **Cyrus the Great**, the son of **Cambyses,** a Persian nobleman, and **Mandane,** the daughter of **Astyages,** king of Media. According to legend, Astyages had a dream that his grandson would become master of Asia and so he tried unsuccessfully to have Cyrus killed when he was still a baby. When he reached manhood, Cyrus defeated his grandfather in battle and went on to fulfill much of the old man's prophecy. Cyrus also subdued the **Lydian Empire,** conquered Babylon and captured all of the Greek cities in Asia Minor. At the same time, he released the Hebrew people held captive in Persia as described in the **Bible** (II Chronicles 36:22-23 and Ezra 1:1-4).

Cyrus the Great.

By the time of his death, Cyrus had created a Persian Empire that stretched from the Hindu Kush Mountains in what is now Afghanistan to the Indus River to the shores of the Mediterranean, where his successors would find themselves facing the Greeks in a contest that would shape the future of world history.

Through Cyrus's conquests, the richness of Persian culture was spread to much of the then-developed world. In his last military campaign against the Scythian Massgetae, his troops were defeated and he was slain. The famous Baroque painter **Peter Paul Reubens (1577-1640)** immortalized Cyrus's final humiliation in his painting *The Head of Cyrus Brought to Queen Tomyris.*

The tomb of Cyrus.

The man who is remembered today as perhaps the greatest of Chinese philosophers was born in what is now the Shantung Province. As a young man, he studied history and archaeology and once visited **Lao Tsu** (see page 12) when

The I Ching.

the latter was the court archivist in the Honan Province. Though influenced by Lao Tsu and **Taoism, Kung Fu-Tzu** decided to follow an alternate path with the goal of becoming a courteous and scholarly gentleman. Philosophically, he was less concerned with an afterlife than the Hindus and Taoists and more concerned with harmonious relations between individual persons, people within the family and people within society.

Pursuing a career as a court philosopher, Kung admonished Chinese rulers to "lead by inner virtue" to win the respect of their subjects and to set an example and permit people to regulate themselves by following that example. He likened a person of authority to the wind, gently influencing those under his command as the wind influences grasses in a field.

As a historical writer, Kung collected poems, stories and legends and combined them into a series of books that still survive as classics of Chinese literature. Among them are the *Book of Odes,* the *Book of Tradition,* the *Book of Rites* and the *Book of Changes* (the *I Ching*).

After his death, his writings continued to be widely read and very influential, and he was eventually discovered by Europeans, who published his works under the latinized name **Confucius.**

Confucianism as a religion is now practiced by five million people, most of them in Asia. As such, it is the sixth most widely followed faith in the world, although it is really more of an ethical system than a religion. The principles of Confucianism include the **Universal Virtues** of benevolence, courtesy and wisdom, and the **Eight Ideals** of filial piety, good faith, integrity, locality, propriety, respect, righteousness and sense of shame.

Confucius.

XERXES I
519-465 BC

In the sixth century BC, **Cyrus the Great** (see page 14) had created the Persian Empire, and his grandson **Darius (558-486 BC)**, who ascended the throne in 521 BC, consolidated Persian rule over Egypt and added the Phoenician fleet to his forces. His next goal was then to conquer

Xerxes I.

Greece by playing upon the internal disagreements among the Greek city-states, but they were able to set aside their differences and unite their forces to turn back his armies. Though outnumbered by the Persians, the better-trained Greeks defeated them at the **Battle of Marathon** in 490 BC.

Ten years later, Darius' eldest son **Xerxes I** (Zûrk′ sēz′) gathered an even larger army. Supported by naval units, the Persian forces marched on Greece in 480 BC with an estimated 2.5 million troops. He overwhelmed **Lenidas,** king of Sparta, at **Thermopylae** and advanced into the Greek heartland. His campaign stumbled on September 23, 480 BC, when the Greeks lured the Persian fleet into the narrow straits off the island of **Salamis**, outmaneuvered it and destroyed it. Xerxes regrouped over the winter and returned the following year and met the Greeks in battle on the **Plain of Plataea**. Again, as had been the case at Marathon and Salamis, an outnumbered Greek force succeeded in outmaneuvering and defeating the larger and more powerful Persian army. Xerxes himself was assassinated in 465 BC and was succeeded by his son **Artaxerxes**, who was never able to recapture the glory days of his father's rule.

Xerxes' defeat at Plataea marked the beginning of the end of the Persian Empire. No longer expanding, it began to collapse from within, and by the end of the next century it was ripe for conquest by Greek armies under **Alexander the Great** (see page23).

Although no one could imagine it at the time, the campaign that had its climax in the Battle of Plataea would prove to be one of the most important turning points in world history. Had Xerxes prevailed, Greece would have fallen under Persian influence, and Persian, rather than Greek, literature would have in turn formed the basis for Western thought.

10. PERICLES
500-429 BC

Born into the nobility, **Pericles** had a pronounced gift for public speaking and entered politics in 469 BC on the side of democracy. He outmaneuvered his rival **Thucydides (c. 460-400 BC)** and eventually became the ruler of **Athens,** the most powerful of the Greek city-states, and brought it to the peak of its glory.

Pericles has been called the greatest constitutional statesman of ancient times, and indeed his list of accomplishments is quite impressive. He built the Athenian fleet into one of the greatest in the world and led the Athenian army in many battles, attacking Delphi and putting down revolts in Euboea and Samos. He adorned Athens with numerous grand public buildings, including the **Parthenon,** and introduced a truly democratic political system in which anyone could hold public office. He also initiated salaries for civil servants and allowances for the poor.

Pericles' mistress, **Aspasia of Miletus (c. 470-410 BC)**, renowned for her beauty and political insight, was a patron of the great philosopher **Socrates (469-399 BC)**

Pericles.

and a valued partner during Pericles' rule. Thanks in no small part to Aspasia's influence upon Pericles, Athens entered its golden age and became the focus of art and culture in the eastern Mediterranean.

Athens' rise to prominence was also facilitated by a peace treaty concluded in 445 BC with the **Peloponnesian Confederacy** headed by the rival city-state of **Sparta.** However, Sparta broke the treaty in 431 BC, setting off three decades of conflict known as the **Peloponnesian War.** After this, Athens never again enjoyed the level of radiance that it had enjoyed under Pericles.

The Parthenon in Athens was built during Pericles' reign.

While many men can be said to have *shaped* history, one man can be said to have *created* it. **Herodotus** developed the means by which we in the Western world record and evaluate history and its milestones. Born in Halicarnassus in Asia Minor, he played a role in the revolution against the tyrant **Lygdamis** and later moved to Athens. It was here that he began to systematically record the history of his own times—in particular the wars between Greece and Persia—and the events that preceded them. While current events had been recorded by others before, Herodotus is considered the first to attempt an orderly and objective study of the interrelation between historical events. Known as the **Father of History,** Herodotus traveled to Egypt and throughout the Mediterranean, where he studied his own as well as foreign cultures and recorded facts as faithfully as he could. In theorizing about history, he applied the traditional Greek idea of the **golden mean,** a notion that held moderation and balance as desirable, with excess and imbalance seen as a prescription for disaster. By this theory, the arrogant **Xerxes I** (see page 16) was inevitably doomed to defeat.

Later in his life, Herodotus helped found the Greek settlement of **Thurii** in Italy where he presumably died.

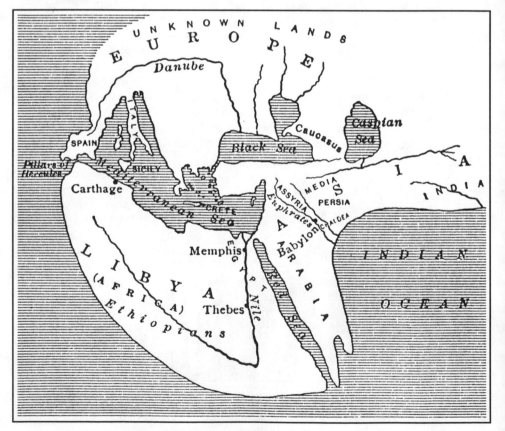

A map of the known world according to Herodotus.

12. SOCRATES
469-399 BC

Born in Athens, **Socrates** was the first of a succession of three great Greek philosophers who today are considered to be the founding fathers of Western philosophical thought. He taught **Plato** (see page 21), who in turn instructed **Aristotle** (see page 22).

Socrates believed that humans existed for a purpose and that right and wrong played a crucial role in defining one's relationships with the environment and other people. As a lecturer, he is remembered for his wit as well as his intellect. Most of what we know about him comes from Plato's *Dialogues,* in which conversations between the two men on philosophical subjects are recorded. Socrates believed that virtue derived from self-knowledge, that people were basically honest, and that evil was a misguided effort to enrich one's own condition. His maxim was "Know thyself."

Socrates believed that the ideal government involved wise men, properly prepared, that ruled for the good of society. He is also remembered for conceiving systematic ideas on the study of the natural harmony of the environment that led to the development of the scientific method.

He believed in the idea of a single unified and transcendent force behind the natural world, an opinion that contradicted the conventional belief in a pantheon of gods. This eventually led to his arrest on charges of corrupting the youth of Athens. His trial is described in Plato's *Apology,* and the *Phaedo* describes his subsequent conversations with his students while he was in jail. After his conviction, he was allowed to commit suicide by drinking hemlock. Though his actual writings are scarce, his life and work live on in the writings of both Plato and **Xenophon (430-357 BC).**

Socrates took his own life by drinking hemlock.

Born on the island of Cos, the son of a Greek physician named **Heraclides, Hippocrates** (hĭ-pŏk′rə-tēz) followed in his father's footsteps in the pursuit of a medical career. He also wrote over 100 books and monographs that influenced medical practice for centuries. Hippocrates was decidedly ahead of his time. In an era when most of the world's medical problems were treated by shamans and witch doctors, he wrote numerous texts on medicine and medical ethics, advancing ideas that were more like those of the twentieth century than of a doctor practicing in the fourth century BC.

He is best remembered for having originated the notion that in curing the sick, a doctor should "consider the nature of humans in general, and of each individual and the characteristics of each disease." In other words, a doctor should consider the interrelationship within the entire human mechanism rather than simply focusing on specific symptoms.

Hippocrates recognized that broken parts must be aligned for normal mending. Traction had to be applied to both ends of a fracture, then released, gradually, as the parts fitted together. As always, he urged the doctor to look beyond the local fracture to the patient's total reaction. Mobilization was recommended at an early stage, since "exercise strengthens and inactivity wastes." Today, this maxim is still followed in the doctor's attempt to avoid "atrophy of disuse."

Scientifically, Hippocrates' work was fairly limited. His ideas about blood circulation, for example, were simply wrong. However, whereas he left most scientific discoveries for later generations, he did formulate the theoretical base and the methods and procedures by which medicine would evolve over the coming centuries. Indeed, Hippocrates literally constructed the framework of modern medical practice. The **Hippocratic Oath,** which he wrote, is still the cornerstone of modern medical ethics. Included within the Hippocratic Oath are such basic tenets as doctor-patient confidentiality, a doctor's responsibilities regarding his patients and a doctor's duty to treat anyone, regardless of their status in society.

Hippocrates.

The most influential of **Socrates'** (see page 19) students, **Plato** was born into the Athenian aristocracy, the son of **Perictione** and her husband **Ariston,** who was descended from **Codrus,** the last king of Athens.

Plato enlisted to fight in the **Peloponnesian War (431-404 BC)** and returned home at age 20 to study with Socrates. He was 28 when his teacher died and he went on to record much of what is known about the teachings of Socrates.

Traveling widely in Babylonia, Egypt, Libya and the Greek colonies in southern Italy, Plato shunned politics but served as court philosopher with **Dionysius of Syracuse,** as well as his brother-in-law and successor, **Dion.** In 353 BC, Plato returned to Athens and founded his Academy, where he taught a small number of specially selected students, among them **Aristotle** (see page 22).

Philosophically, Plato perpetuated and elaborated upon many of Socrates' ideas. In *The Republic,* he proposed a "perfect state in which ethics, virtue and reason are in balance." Like Socrates, he was a proponent of the pursuit of wisdom rather than the acceptance of dogma.

Plato was also one of the earliest male advocates of women's rights. He believed that women had an equal place in government and civic life, and in an age when women were not privy to higher education, he supported their access to learning as a means for them to prepare for civic responsibilities.

Also like his great teacher, Plato believed that universal truths embodied virtue and harmony. He believed in the ideal forms of beauty, truth and goodness and that such forms followed from a quest for knowledge and wisdom.

In the third century AD, Plato's ideas were revived by the **Neoplatonic Movement** led by **Plotinus,** and later through the work of **St. Thomas Aquinas** (see page 38). They greatly influenced the philosophic basis of Christianity as it emerged from the **Middle Ages.**

The great philosopher Plato.

15. ARISTOTLE
384-322 BC

Taught by **Plato** (see page 21) and the teacher of **Alexander the Great** (see page 23), **Aristotle** was one of history's greatest philosophers, and was one of the first to fully explore the relationship and synergy of all aspects of nature and humanity. He studied and lectured upon poetry, astronomy and biology, as well as on metaphysics, aesthetics and logic.

Born in Stagira, a Greek outpost on the Macedonian coast, Aristotle became a pupil of Plato at age 17, remaining first as a student and later as a teacher at Plato's Academy in Athens for 20 years. It was during this period that he taught Alexander. Aristotle left the Academy after Plato's death, but when Alexander came to power in 336 BC, he returned to Athens. Under Alexander's auspices, he formed his own school, the **Lyceum,** which he headed until 323 BC.

The Aristotelian philosophy which evolved during this time included his six treatises on logic, which are considered to be his most important work, as well as treatises on metaphysics, physics, ethics, politics and natural sciences. In the case of the latter, he was one of the first to collect and systematically classify biological specimens. This is descriptive of Aristotle's propensity for careful analysis and the tracing of natural "laws" or the balances that governed nature. Plato had postulated the theory of ideal **forms,** and Aristotle theorized further that matter could not be without form because it exists. He suggested that the perfect, pure or ultimate form was that which he called **theos,** or what we know as God.

In politics, Aristotle believed that the *ideal* was a blend of democracy and monarchy.

Aristotle also studied medicine as well as philosophy and science. It can be said that his major impact on the evolution of

Aristotle.

learning was his application of a systematic method to the study of human relationships with other aspects of the world around it.

Aristotelian thought was ultimately harmonized with Christian theology by **St. Thomas Aquinas** (see page 38) in the thirteenth century, with Jewish theology by **Maimonides (1135-1204)** and with Islam by **Averroes (1126-1198).**

Alexander was the son of **Philip II of Macedonia** and **Olympias,** the daughter of Neptolemus of Epirus. Philip, himself a great leader, had brought all of Greece under his rule just before his assassination in 336 BC. Young Alexander grew up in Athens, not only in the shadow of his father but of the great philosopher Aristotle, who was his teacher. He succeeded his father at age 20, already a man destined for greatness. Although Alexander ruled for only 13 years, during this time he was able to build an empire greater than any that had yet existed.

He was destined to do what the Persians had failed to do a century before: He established a vast empire that straddled both Europe and Asia and stretched from Greece to India. This is why we know him as **Alexander the Great.**

After he defeated the Persian emperor **Darius III (558-486 BC)** in the **Battle of Issus** in 333 BC, the Persian Empire crumbled. By the time he was 33, Alexander ruled 50 times as much land and 20 times as many people as had existed in the empire he inherited from Philip. This territory included Greece, Egypt, all of the former Persian Empire and all of what we think of

today as the Middle East. He had marched as far north as the Danube in Europe, as far east as the Ganges in India, and he had even sent an expedition deep into Africa to find the source of the Nile River.

Upon Alexander's death in 323 BC, he was considered to have been the greatest general and empire-builder the world had ever known. Even today, almost two dozen centuries later, he has barely half a dozen rivals to this achievement.

Although Alexander was a brilliant, charismatic leader, the true importance of Alexander's empire was that, for the first time, there could be a free exchange of ideas between the different cultures in two vast regions that had previously been isolated from one another. Unlike most other victorious leaders, Alexander was not only receptive to the ideas of his conquered peoples but adopted ideas he learned from Persian political organization. On the other hand, Greek art influenced the art of India. Before his untimely death of natural causes at age 33, Alexander also built the city of **Alexandria** in Egypt, whose great library survived for a thousand years and evolved into the greatest center of learning in the world.

Alexander leading his army.

23

By definition, a leader is able to lead because of a distinct mixture of intelligence and power that we call "leadership." In the early days of human civilization, leaders were seen as more omnipotent and separate from the people they ruled, and many were thought to have divine powers. In Egypt, for example, the pharaohs had been accepted as being gods themselves. The authority of kings was enormous and they typically ruled by decree. What the king dictated became the law of the land. Some rulers were benevolent and some were arbitrarily cruel, but most ruled with an iron hand. To do otherwise would be to invite disrespect.

Asoka was perhaps history's first major exception to this rule.

Asoka was born a member of the **Maurya Dynasty** in what is now India sometime before 300 BC, and he ruled the kingdom of Magadha from 273 BC to 232 BC. His empire eventually came to include almost all of what is India today (except the southern tip), as well as what is now Pakistan, Bangladesh and part of Afghanistan. In 261 BC, his armies crushed the **Kalingas** in a particularly bloody war which had up to 200,000 casualties. As a witness to the horror and suffering, Asoka was appalled and decided that no military victory was worth such a cost. He converted to Buddhism and renounced military conquest as a national policy. He banned animal and human sacrifice and retained his army in a solely defensive posture.

Asoka had become a man with a conscience, and possibly the world's first truly "enlightened" monarch. He was perhaps the first to alter this pattern. Beyond simply reacting to the violence of aggressive foreign policy, he also reformulated his domestic policy to include public works projects and the establishment of institutions that would serve the welfare of the people he governed.

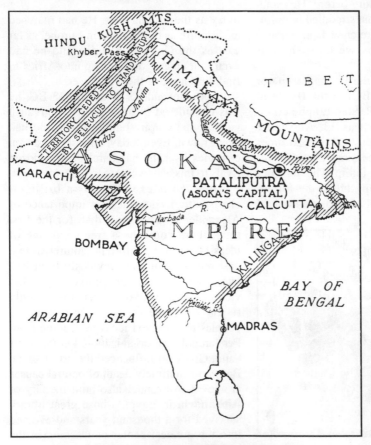

A map showing the extent of Asoka's empire.

Perhaps the greatest mathematician to live before the **Renaissance, Archimedes** was born in Syracuse on the island of Sicily and studied science under **Conon of Samos** at the University of **Alexandria** during that city's golden age as a world center of learning. Archimedes devised many of the basic theorems involving the geometry of circles, cones, cylinders, parabolas, planes and spheres, which constitute the basic building blocks of **mathematics.**

The great mathematician Archimedes.

After studying astronomy, Archimedes constructed a spherical, three-dimensional "map" of the heavens. He also completed a great deal of pioneering work in the field of physics, writing extensively on such basic machines as the **lever,** the **pulley** and the **screw.** He was so successful in his study of the application of the lever that he once boasted, "Give me a place to stand and I can move the Earth [with a lever]."

One of Archimedes' most important mechanical inventions was the **Archimedean screw.** Designed as a rotating pump to raise water from streams into irrigation ditches, the screw was immersed in a water source at a shallow angle so that the lowest part of any given thread was lower than the highest part of the thread below it. When the shaft of the screw was rotated about its axis so that the threads screwed into the water, water was lifted up the spiral and discharged from the top of the thread.

Archimedes also invented the science of **Hydrostatics,** which is the study of fluid dynamics. While sitting in his bath one day, he discovered the principle of **displacement,** which states that a solid immersed in liquid loses weight by an amount equal to that of the liquid being displaced.

When the Romans attacked Syracuse in 214 BC, Archimedes designed a number of useful defense weapons, from long-range catapults to mirrors that used the Sun to set fire to Roman ships. When the Romans finally invaded the city two years later, Archimedes was ordered spared. However, when a Roman foot soldier interfered with some calculations that Archimedes was sketching on the ground with a stick and Archimedes shouted at him, the soldier killed the great man on the spot. When he heard what had happened, the Roman general Marcellus erected a tomb in the mathematician's honor.

Shih Huang Ti conceived, and began work on, the **Great Wall of China,** the greatest engineering project undertaken by human hands prior to the nineteenth century. He was also the first leader to completely unify the nation which is today the world's most populous. In the history of China, he is known as the **First Emperor.**

Like Europe before and after the peak of the Roman Empire's power, China was a conglomeration of politically divergent feudal city-states ruled by rival warlords. These states were united only by a generally common culture that had emerged during the **Chou Dynasty,** which originated in the Yangtze River Valley after 770 BC and exerted a lasting cultural, if not political, influence on the rest of China.

The teachings of **Confucius (Kung Fu-Tsu)** (see page 15) had also exerted a powerful influence on Chinese culture during this period. His philosophy, still followed as a religion by 5.2 million people, stressed the importance of a harmonious social order on a national, as well as personal, level. However, after his death, China disintegrated politically into the **Warring States Period (about 403-221 BC).**

The Warring States Period ended with the advent of the **Chin Dynasty (221-210 BC),** during which Shih Huang Ti succeeded in uniting China for the first time in history. He introduced a centralized government, conducted a census and standardized the country's coinage, written language, laws, and weights and measures. On the down side, Shih Huang Ti was also an authoritarian despot who undertook a concerted effort to stamp out Confucianism, an objective at which he was only partially successful.

In order to consolidate his rule and to protect China from the Mongols of Central Asia, Shih ordered construction of the Great Wall of China. This massive wall eventually stretched 1500 miles, was punctuated with permanently manned guard towers and made it possible for Shih's single, unified China to survive.

Shih's rule was superseded by the **Han Dynasty,** which continued Shih's centralization of government but gradually reintroduced Confucianism. The Han Dynasty went on to establish the **Mandarin** social and political system, which survived as the basis of Chinese society even under the **Ch'ing (Manchu) Dynasty (1644-1912)** until the Communists seized power in 1949.

The Great Wall of China was conceived by Shih Huang Ti.

With the defeat of **Carthage** in the **Punic Wars (264-146 BC),** Rome dominated the Mediterranean and Roman leaders came to think of Rome as having a "manifest destiny" to subjugate and rule as much of the known world as possible. It was through **Gaius Julius Caesar** that Rome actually realized this manifest destiny by extending the frontiers of the **Roman Empire** farther than any Roman emperor ever had before. Immortalized in story, verse and on the Shakespearean stage, he is recalled as the quintessential Roman emperor, although Rome was still a republic when he was alive and the office of emperor wasn't created until after his death.

Caesar, the son of a noble family, entered the Roman army and served in Asia with distinction, earning the **Civic Crown,** the highest medal of valor. Upon his return to Rome, he entered politics, became state treasurer at age 34, chief preistat at 39 and was elected to a consulship at age 43.

In order to enhance the power and glory of Rome as well as his own fame, Caesar undertook a successful military expedition to the north. Between 58 and 55 BC, he conquered Gaul (present day France), Helvetii (Switzerland) and Belgica (Belgium). He also invaded and laid claim to most of Britain and crossed the Rhine River to fight the Germans.

Caesar returned to Rome a hero but encountered a political conflict with **Pompey (106-48 BC),** the Roman general who had captured Jerusalem. Pompey also held the post of Chief Consul and had married Caesar's daughter, **Julia.** Caesar demanded the consulship for himself, but it was given to Pompey.

By law, generals were not allowed to bring their armies into the city of Rome but rather were required to keep them north of the Rubicon River. In 50 BC, Caesar

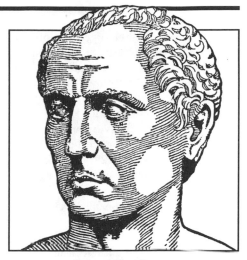

Gaius Julius Caesar.

flaunted this law, crossed the Rubicon and entered Rome to stage a coup. He deposed Pompey and eliminated the republic, making himself an absolute ruler as he had always planned. After he consolidated Roman rule over Greece and led a campaign of conquest into Syria and Egypt, he returned to Rome in 46 BC to be declared perpetual dictator of Rome and rule as the greatest world conqueror in history, greater even than **Alexander the Great** (see page 23).

Caesar continued to rule until he was assassinated in the Roman Senate by **Marcus Junius Brutus (85-42 BC),** a disgruntled colleague, on March 15, 44 BC.

Julius Caesar greatly altered the course of Roman—and indeed, of European—history. In Rome itself, he had overthrown the republic and created the office of a de facto emperor, which his nephew **Caesar Augustus** (see page 28) made official when he took power 14 years after his uncle's death. When Caesar had begun his rise to power, Rome was the major political force in the Mediterranean. By the time of his death, Rome had also become Europe's—and possibly the world's—first superpower.

21. CAESAR AUGUSTUS (OCTAVIAN) 63 BC-14 AD

Caesar Augustus.

Julius Caesar had enlarged the boundaries of what was a de facto **Roman Empire,** and he had become Rome's first absolute ruler. Yet the Roman Empire was not officially declared until his nephew **Octavian** took power in 27 BC. He was the son of **Caius Octavius** and his wife **Atia,** whose mother was **Julia,** sister of **Julius Caesar** (see page 27). Octavian was 30 years old when his uncle was assassinated.

Although Caesar had named Octavian as his successor, the younger man faced opposition from both his uncle's supporters and his rivals. Octavian agreed to rule as part of a **triumvirate** (a three-man ruling council) with **Marcus Lepidus (?- 13 BC)** and **Mark Antony (83-30 BC),** the latter being one of Caesar's trusted lieutenants. This triumvirate in turn faced a civil war brought about by **Gaius Cassius (?-42 BC)** and **Marcus Junius Brutus (85-42 BC),** two of the conspirators in Caesar's assassination who wanted to re-establish the republic. After their defeat, the triumvirate divided their rule geographically, with Octavian in Europe, Lepidus in Africa and Antony in Egypt.

In Egypt, where the local monarchy was subject to Roman rule, Mark Antony set up his seat of power in the cosmopolitan city of Alexandria, where he fell in love with and married the Egyptian queen **Cleopatra (69-30 BC).** He named their three children as his successors and frequently gave his wife lavish presents, which spawned a rumor that he planned to give her Rome itself as a gift. When word of this rumor reached Octavian, he became infuriated and immediately declared war. The two sides met in the **Battle of Actium** in 31 BC, and the armies of Antony and Cleopatra were defeated, after which they fled to Egypt with the remnants of their forces, with Octavian in close pursuit. Sensing that their cause was hopeless, both Antony and Cleopatra committed suicide in 30 BC.

Octavian returned to Rome in 29 BC and declared himself to be the Roman emperor, taking the name **Caesar Augustus.** Under his rule, the Roman Empire became a tightly disciplined, centrally controlled monarchy, and he made the Latin language and the Roman alphabet a standard for all of Europe. Although Rome had been an empire before Octavian became Caesar Augustus, it was he who proclaimed it to be *the* Roman Empire, and it was he who presided over a period when *Pax Romana* (the peace of Rome) reigned throughout the "known world."

United under a single strong leader, the Roman Empire began to prosper both culturally and commercially. Art and literature became an important part of life in Roman cities, and massive construction projects were undertaken to build roads, bridges, aqueducts, coliseums, apartment houses and public buildings in the city of Rome and throughout the Empire. It has been said that Octavian inherited a Rome built of brick and left a Rome built of marble.

22. JESUS CHRIST
4 BC–29 AD

Born in a stable in Bethlehem in what was then Roman Palestine, **Jesus Christ** founded what has come to be the world's most widely followed religion. Today there are 1.6 billion Christians in the world, accounting for just under one-third of the world's people. He was born to **Mary** and her husband **Joseph,** a carpenter from Nazareth. Orthodox Christians believe that Joseph was simply his stepfather because Jesus was, literally, the **Son of God.**

Jesus began teaching when he was 29 years of age after being introduced to the people of the region by his cousin **John (St. John the Baptist),** a prophet who identified Jesus as the Son of God and the **Messiah.** Jesus' most well-known message, the **Sermon on the Mount,** summarizes the essence of Christian belief in a moral code that teaches the importance of peace, honesty, simplicity, tolerance and meekness.

The Jewish tradition—into which Jesus was born—was unique among ancient religions in its belief that there was only one god. The Jews further believed that their one god—known as **Jehovah**—would send a messiah, or savior, to deliver them from Roman rule as Moses had delivered them from Egyptian slavery about 1250 BC. Christians not only believe that Jesus was that Messiah, but also that he is the Son of God who was sent to give his life for the people of Earth in order for them to be reborn in God's grace and have access to eternal paradise, or heaven. To Chris-

tians, the birth of Jesus Christ was the pivotal event of world history.

Christians adopted Jewish scriptures for the period prior to 4 BC and these form the *Old Testament* of the Christian **Bible.** The two traditions diverge at that point, as Jews do not accept that Jesus Christ was *the* Messiah. The *New Testament* of the Bible contains a record of Christ's own teaching as recorded by his disciples, mainly Matthew, Mark, Luke and John.

During the years that he was preaching in Palestine, Jesus worked numerous miracles and attracted many followers. He also made enemies in official circles among those who saw the charismatic preacher as a threat to their authority. In 29 or 30 AD, Jesus was arrested in Jerusalem and sentenced to death by the Roman prosecutor **Pontius Pilate.** Jesus was nailed to a cross on a hill called Calvary and left to die. According to Christian belief, his body—united with his soul—rose from the dead three days later, and he appeared to his followers many times over the next 40 days. These followers then set out to preach his words to the people of the Roman Empire and the world beyond.

Children receiving the teaching of Christ.

After the death of **Caesar Augustus (Octavian)** (see page 28), Imperial Rome prospered as no society on Earth had before. The Roman Empire was secure and its military power unchallenged. It was against this backdrop of civil order and relative peace that Christianity began to grow and expand. Unlike previous religions, Christianity actively sought to convert others. It took root in the Middle East and spread to Greece and Egypt.

Originally known as **Saul, St. Paul** was born in Tarsus in what is now southern Turkey. A tent-maker by trade, he also studied philosophy in Jerusalem and spoke several languages, including Greek.

At first Saul was quite hostile to Christian doctrine, but shortly after the crucifixion of **Jesus Christ** (see page 29), Christ appeared to him in a vision while he was riding on the road to Damascus. Converted to Christianity on the spot, Saul changed his name to Paul and answered Christ's call to preach his word to the world.

According to the **Bible** (Galacians 1:18, 19), Paul went to Jerusalem and met with Christ's disciples **Peter, James** and **Barnabus.** It was during these and subsequent meetings that they worked out a plan to spread Christ's teachings to the Middle East and beyond. For the next 10 years, Paul himself—alone or with Barnabus—traveled to Tarsus, Greece, Macedonia and Cyprus to establish churches. In the course of his travels, Paul wrote letters, or **epistles,** detailing Christian doctrine.

Paul's missionary work met with little success in Athens, but he went on to Corinth where he spent about 18 months around 58 AD. It was here that he wrote his **Letters to the Corinthians,** considered to be some of his most important work.

Over the next several years, Paul's success brought the wrath of both Jewish and Roman authorities upon him because he

St. Paul preaching in Athens.

had converted both Jews and non-Jews to Christianity. Although non-Jews were, of course, exempt from Jewish law, Jewish leaders in Jerusalem believed that Jewish Christians should not be exempt. When Paul entered the debate, he was jailed for two years.

Upon his release, Paul went to Rome. The story of his voyage, which involved being shipwrecked on the island of Malta, is an amazing tale that is recounted by St. Luke (Acts 27:1-28:16). In Rome, he met with **St. Peter,** the friend and hand-picked successor of Jesus, and was welcomed into the Christian community where he spent two fruitful years writing and lecturing. He was said to have been planning a trip to Spain, but he probably had not yet gone when he was arrested and executed by the emperor, **Nero (37-68 AD)** in 67 AD.

Whereas St. Peter was the first pope of the Christian Church, St. Paul was—after Jesus himself—probably the most influential figure in the establishment of Christianity and the systematic foundation of Christian doctrine.

24. CONSTANTINE
280-337 AD

Constantine became the Emperor of Rome in 306 AD when his father, **Constantius Chlorus,** died at York. He came to power at a time of domestic discontent and faced a crumbling Roman Empire, from which even parts of Italy wanted to secede. He fought numerous battles with his rivals, culminating in his defeat of **Licinius** at Chrysopolis and at Adnianople in 323 AD.

Meanwhile, Christianity had at first been tolerated by the Romans, but as it became more widespread and a threat was perceived, emperors began to persecute the Christians. The ugly spectacle of Christians being thrown to the lions in Rome's coliseum for the amusement of Roman crowds became a familiar sight.

During the battle at Adnianople, Constantine reportedly witnessed a cross in a vision. Crediting **Jesus Christ** (see page 29) with his victory, he embraced Christianity as a state religion. Before Constantine, Christianity had been subject to persecution, but after 323 AD, it was accepted and even promoted.

Constantine even went so far as to mediate a major internal dispute over doctrine between the eastern and western factions of the church. He invited the bishops representing the two groups to a huge conference in Nicaea in 325 AD, at which their differences were resolved. The **Nicaean Creed,** drafted at this meeting, set out the basic Christian beliefs upon which both sides could agree. Constantine then es-

Constantine.

tablished Christianity as a de facto state religion throughout the Roman Empire.

Constantine took steps to save Christianity from being destroyed by either external persecution or internal strife. He not only preserved Christianity, he took an all-important step toward making it the dominant religion in Europe.

Christians of Constantine's era.

Born the son of a pagan father and **St. Monica (333-387 AD)** in Tagaste in what is now Algeria, **Augustine** entered the University of Carthage at age 16, and at age 20 he wrote of his "incredible thirst for the immortality of wisdom."

Augustine turned to the Christian scriptures and started a school to instruct students in writing and grammar. In 383 AD, he traveled to Rome and later to Milan to study and teach. After a great deal of study, he converted to Christianity, and in 387 AD he was baptized by his religious studies teacher, **St. Ambrose (340-397 AD).**

After Augustine returned to Africa, he devoted himself solely to religious studies, and in 391 AD he was ordained as a priest. Four years later, he accepted the post of **Bishop of Hippo,** a position he held until his death 39 years later. During his lifetime, his writings assured him a place as perhaps the greatest theologian in Christian history. He reconciled the philosophy of **Plato** (see page 21) with Christian theology and published several important works, including *City of God* (c. 426 AD) and the treatise *Confessions* (c. 399 AD), which dealt with the balance of good and evil in the world and the inherent goodness of all beings created by God.

Like Plato and so many other great philosophers, Augustine had a passionate desire to make contact with a reality that transcended that which could be perceived by the senses. He believed that a blend of faith and reason was a necessary precursor to knowledge, and that human reason, though capable of considering and appreciating God, was not necessarily able to fully understand Him. Augustine spent a great deal of time contemplating the nature of God and God's relationship to time and space. He concluded that God was the catalyst for all change in the universe and that while God was always present and had al-

St. Augustine.

ways been present, He occupied no specific physical space and did not exist in time. God had in fact existed before the creation of the universe and therefore had existed before there was time.

Augustine was living in Hippo when the **Vandals** besieged the city in May 430 AD. Three months later, on August 28, he was killed, but his legacy would live on as a major cornerstone of Christian theology.

The founder of the religious faith known as **Islam, Mohammed** was born around 570 AD near Mecca in what is now Saudi Arabia. His parents died when he was young and Mohammed was raised by other family members. When he was still a boy, he traveled throughout the Middle East with his uncle who was a trader, coming into contact with many different people and becoming familiar with their ideas and customs. He was attracted to the Judeo-Christian idea of monotheism.

In 610 AD, while he was meditating near **Mecca,** he began to experience a series of visions in which God instructed him to preach monotheism to the polytheistic peoples of the Arabian peninsula. He also began work on the **Koran,** Islam's sacred scripture. As he gained disciples to his faith, the authorities in Mecca began to perceive him as a threat to their authority. Finally, they surrounded Mohammed and many of his followers in one corner of the city and threatened to let them starve to death unless Mohammed retracted what he had been preaching and his followers abandon Mohammed and monotheism.

By this time, two rival factions in neighboring **Medina** had taken an interest in Mohammed and his beliefs and invited him to come there. He escaped from Mecca on July 16, 622 AD and went to Medina. This date of Mohammed's journey, or hejira (hĕ-jərə), marks the beginning of Islam.

Having been embraced by the rulers of Medina, Mohammed raised an army to use in spreading Islamic beliefs to rival tribes. He returned to conquer Mecca in 630 AD, and by the time of his death in 632 AD, his armies had "converted" most of the people on the Arabian peninsula.

Within 10 years of Mohammed's death, this process had been extended to Persia, Egypt and throughout the Middle East. By the middle of the eighth century, the territory, controlled both politically and religiously by the Islamic Empire, stretched from Spain across North Africa through the Middle East and into Central Asia. Today, Islam is the second most widely held religious belief in the world, with over 800 million faithful, accounting for 17 percent of the world's people. Like Judaism and Christianity, Islam is monotheistic. The followers of Islam believe in one God, whom they call **Allah.** As the Muslims say, "There is no God but Allah, and Mohammed is the messenger of God."

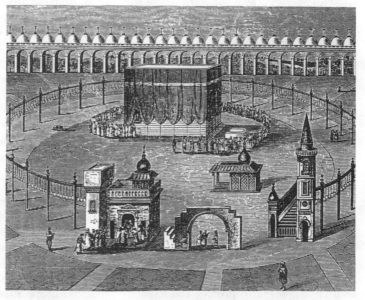

The Kaaba at Mecca is an important Islamic holy site.

27. CHARLEMAGNE
742-814 AD

The Roman Empire had been the dominant political reality in Europe and the Mediterranean for half a millennium when it and collapsed in 476 AD. Europe had lost the unity of the Roman Empire that had been present for generations upon generations, and became a patchwork of squabbling kingdoms. Fragments of the former whole empire became individual power centers ruled by various monarchs. However, even as Europe was fragmented politically it was unified religiously by the common bond of Christianity, and this became a principle characteristic of life in the period we now refer to as the **Middle Ages.**

While the home of the Christian popes in Rome remained the spiritual center of Europe, the Franks in northern Europe emerged as the strongest military and secular power. By the end of the eighth century, their most powerful leader was the 26-year-old **Charlemagne** (the French word for **Charles the Great**), the son of **Pepin the Short (714?-768 AD)** and grandson of **Charles Martel (789?-741 AD),** whom we now consider to be one of the greatest rulers in European history. Even the mightiest rulers face opposition, and Charlemagne's principal opponent was the Italian king **Desiderius,** who wanted Pope **Adrian I** to crown the underage children of Charlemagne's predecessor as monarchs of segments of the kingdom of the Franks.

After Charlemagne defeated Desiderius, he consolidated most of the states of northern Italy under Frank control. He then went to Rome to meet with the pope and found that their long-range strategies were quite compatible. Charlemagne's goal was to become head of an empire on the scale of the old Roman Empire, and Adrian I wanted one dominant, unified, political force to rule Europe that would ally itself with the Church and serve to protect and expand Christendom the way the Moorish armies

Charlemagne.

were spreading Islam. With the blessing of the pope, Charlemagne added much of Denmark, Germany and Central Europe to an empire that already included France and most of Italy. He also recaptured part of Spain from the Moors.

On Christmas Day in 800 AD, while he was attending Mass in Rome, Charlemagne unexpectedly found himself being crowned "Emperor of the Romans" by Adrian's successor, **Leo III.** The Western Roman Empire, which had not existed for 325 years, was back in business, this time as the Holy Roman Empire (though it was not yet *officially* known as such). Although he was not recognized by the emperor of the Eastern Roman Empire until 812 AD, Charlemagne quickly won the respect of most of the peoples of his empire, enabling Europe to once again experience the *Pax Romana* of a unified and basically peaceful environment. Because of this, Charlemagne's rule can be said to have been the shining moment in the millennium of turbulence that gripped Europe after the fall of the Roman Empire.

Upon his death, the great empire of **Charlemagne** (see page 34) was inherited by his intended successor, **Louis the Pious (778-840 AD).** After Louis died, infighting among his sons caused the empire to disintegrate. The void was filled by the Catholic Church, which began to assert increasing political as well as spiritual power. Europe, however, had begun to sink back into the Dark Ages. The disunity that preceded Charlemagne's brilliant rule had returned. Although Italy and France were a morass of warring factions, among the Germans, a new leader emerged. **Henry I (876?-936 AD),** known as "The Fowler," was a forceful leader who consolidated the German states, leaving to his son and successor, **Otto I,** a formidable power base.

Otto I sought to bring unity to the lands that had once comprised Charlemagne's vast empire. Again, as it had been with Charlemagne, Otto's authority sprang from the pope's desire for a strong northern Europe that would restore order in Italy. Pope **John XII** was at war with the Italian king **Berengar** and offered Otto the crown and title of Holy Roman Emperor if he would defeat Berengar and unite the Italian peninsula, which he did.

Otto I was crowned on February 2, 962 AD. The idea of a Holy Roman Empire had been born with Charlemagne and now it was reborn with Otto I. Charlemagne's empire survived his death by only 27 years. However, the Holy Roman Empire survived Otto's death by more than eight centuries. Otto's empire essentially consisted of the present territory of Germany, Austria, Italy, the Czech Republic and some adjacent territory. It would continue to wield might and power until the fifteenth century, and it would survive in name until 1806. Just as it was intended, the Holy Roman Empire brought political as well as spiritual union to the heart of Europe by bringing many diverse peoples together.

In the centuries that immediately followed, all the superpowers that appeared—England, France and Spain—were outside of the Holy Roman Empire. The autonomy that remained in individual kingdoms within the Holy Roman Empire prevented the emergence of a true power center in the Empire itself.

Otto I.

Following the collapse of the Roman Empire in the fifth century, Britain, like the rest of this former Empire, became a swirling cauldron of rival political interests. By the ninth century, however, the Anglo-Saxons predominated, ruling the land from 828 to 1016 AD, when the Danes conquered Britain. In 1042, the throne went to a Saxon who had lived most of his life in his mother's native Normandy in northern France. **Edward I (1004?-1066),** also known as **Edward the Confessor,** was the stepson of **Canute (995-1035),** the first Danish king. Edward seized power after his two stepbrothers, Harold I and Harde Canute, served as king for seven years.

Edward the Confessor died in 1066 and was succeeded by his Saxon brother-in-law, King **Harold II (1027-1066).** Although Edward had publicly promised the throne to Harold, he had also made a similar promise in private to his cousin, **William of Normandy.** The son of **Robert the Devil,** the duke of Normandy, and **Arlette,** the daughter of a tanner named Falaise, William succeeded his father in 1035 and visited England in 1051. Assuming that he had a legitimate right to the English throne, he gathered an army of Normans and Frenchmen, crossed the English Channel from Normandy and invaded England. Harold, failing to disrupt his landing, met William in the **Battle of Hastings** on October 14, 1066.

Harold's troops, which were on foot, proved to be a poor match for the more heavily armed and armored Normans who were mounted on horseback. William's cavalry also outmaneuvered the Saxon infantry, and by the end of the day, Harold and many of his officers were dead, their armies defeated. On Christmas Day, William was crowned king of England and was henceforth known as **William the Conqueror.** Although both **Napoleon Bonaparte** (see page 62) and **Adolf Hitler** (see page 97) later tried to duplicate his momentous victory, William was the last man in history to head a victorious invasion of England by a force of arms.

In the wake of William's victory, England was opened to the influences of European art and literature. Although England retained its English language, it filtered and adopted the best that Europe had to offer, and the course of English civilization changed dramatically. This would in turn create and define the civilization of North America.

William the Conqueror.

Born on the Onon River in Mongolia, the son of a chief who had ruled much of Mongolia from the Amur to the **Great Wall of China, Temujin** succeeded his father at the age of 13. However, he did not win a military victory until he defeated the Keraites in 1203. With this, his people declared him **Genghis Khan,** which means "mighty ruler." He took his new title to heart and set out on a campaign of conquest that lasted 25 years.

Genghis first turned his attention to the Tartars. Having defeated them, he plunged south into China, where the **Song Dynasty** was on the brink of ruin and hence an easy target for the marauding Mongols. Genghis captured Beijing in 1214 and soon occupied most of China. For centuries, the Mongols had been a nomadic people who lived on the vast plains of Central Asia. For many years they eked out a living on the steppes, fighting among themselves and raiding villages on the fringes of the Chinese Empire. Few people beyond the periphery of their homeland had even heard of them. The Great Wall of China, begun around 200 BC, generally kept them at bay, and most of Europe was several thousand miles from the cold, high deserts the Mongols inhabited.

Now, neither wall nor distance would matter. In 1219, Genghis Khan looked west toward lands that had not yet heard of his conquests. The **Mongol Hordes,** as the vast waves of heavily armed horsemen came to be known, swept across Russia, digested the Persian Empire, swallowed Poland and Hungary, and threatened all of Europe.

The Mongol warlord who had little use for the finer things of Chinese or European civilization, slept in a yurt and rode a fast, sturdy Mongolian stallion, evolved as perhaps the most successful military leader in the history of the world. Genghis Khan

Genghis Khan.

saw no limit to the potential size of his Mongol Empire. Over the next eight years, he amassed the largest contiguous empire the world had yet seen.

However, the success of the Hordes was completely dependent upon Genghis Khan's leadership abilities and his unification of the Mongols. When **Ogadai Khan** (Ōgə-dī' Kän) **(1185-1241)** succeeded him after his death and continued on a path of conquest, the Mongol juggernaut eventually ran out of steam and the Hordes returned to Asia. In China, the Mongol, or **Yuan Dynasty,** would last until 1368.

The most important impact that Genghis Khan and the Mongol Empire had on history was that it made people at opposite ends of the globe—China and Europe—aware of one another. The **Crusades** had reopened the ancient dialogue between Europe and the Middle East, but before the Mongols, Europeans were largely unaware that the Far East existed.

One of the greatest of Christian philosophers and scholars of all time, **St. Thomas** was born near Roccasecca near Monte Cassino in Italy, the son of the **Count of Aquino.** He studied at the Benedictine monastery at Cassino and went on to the University of Naples, where he was introduced to the works of **Aristotle** (see page 22).

Between 1259 and 1268, St. Thomas studied at the University of the Papal Curia in Italy before setting out to write his commentaries on the *Physics, Metaphysics, Ethics and Politics* of Aristotle and begin work on his own masterpiece, *Summa Theologica* (1242). From Italy he journeyed to Paris, where he taught and worked on the *Unity of Intellect,* which vindicated individualism in thought and personality. He then returned to the University of Naples where he lived until his death. He also spent time in Florence, where he became a strong influence in the early life of the great Italian poet **Dante Alighieri (1265-1321).**

St. Thomas began with Aristotelian definitions and tempered them with the Christian virtues of faith, hope and charity. Philosophically, he was a proponent of **Scholasticism,** which is the harmonizing of faith and reason, and the codification of knowledge in this context. As a philosophical successor to Aristotle in his belief that "form" gives matter its being, he further reasoned that God is the epitome in the hierarchy of forms. He viewed free will as the root of ethics, noting that humans are free in regard to means but not an end; hence, free will is only a means to an end.

St. Thomas believed that divine forces and natural forces were not arbitrary and distinct but harmonious with one another. In *Divine Names,* he wrote that "God is known through all things and yet apart from all things; and He is known through

St. Thomas Aquinas.

knowledge and through ignorance [the absence of knowledge]." One of his most significant contributions to Western thought was his belief that the progress of human civilization has real meaning and that spiritual and intellectual life are extremely valuable in this context.

One of the most profound tributes to St. Thomas's scholarship came in the seventeenth century when the noted French philosopher **Rene Descartes (1596-1650)** undertook a skeptical analysis of theological thought and discovered that St. Thomas had anticipated and answered possible rebuttals to his ideas. St. Thomas alone among the Christian scholars of the **Middle Ages** appeared to have an answer for everything.

Marco Polo was born in the Italian city-state of Venice at a time when Europeans had little or no idea of the people and cultures of China and the rest of east Asia. Europeans had heard that China existed but knew little about Asia beyond what they had heard about **Genghis Khan** and his Mongol Hordes (see page 37) or what they had learned second-hand from traders who had traveled in Turkey or the Middle East.

In the mid-1260s, Marco's father and uncle, **Nicolo Polo** and **Maffeo Polo,** decided that the best way to learn about China was to go there. After a long and difficult trek, they were received at the court of **Kublai Khan (1215-1294),** the Mongol emperor of China, who had never before met a European. Kublai Khan was very interested in what they had to say. He told them to ask the pope to send missionaries to instruct the Chinese people in Christianity and the art and literature of Europe. When the brothers returned home in 1269, their fellow countrymen could not grasp the enormity of their story.

In 1271, they decided to return to China, and this time they took Nicolo's teenage son, Marco. Kublai Khan took a liking to the young man and made him an ambassador at large, sending him on many missions within China, as well as to Tibet and Burma. Eventually, Marco Polo saw more of Asia than any European had ever seen, or even had dreamed of seeing. Along with his father and uncle, he stayed in China for over 20 years, learning the languages and customs of Asia and meeting many of its diverse peoples.

When the Polos returned to Venice in 1295, they once again met with skepticism, but after they demonstrated what they had earned in China, their fellow Venetians were quite impressed, and the Polos were welcomed and honored. Many of the things that they had brought back from China were truly amazing and had never been seen in Europe before. There is even a tale—unproven—that they introduced spaghetti into Italy from China.

Marco's book, *The Travels of Marco Polo,* is perhaps the most famous and influential travel book in history because with its wealth of detail it provided Europeans of the **Middle Ages** with their first substantial knowledge of China and other Asian countries.

Because of the difficulty of traveling over land, trade between Europe and the Far East was slow to develop, but the way was opened after Marco Polo published the details of a workable trade route. His travels of discovery expanded Europe's horizons beyond anything most people could ever have imagined possible. Indeed, the voyages of **Christopher Columbus** (see page 41) two centuries later were also inspired by the desire to find a shorter, easier route to the riches of China.

Marco Polo.

Born in Mainz, Germany, with the surname **Gensfleisch, Johann Gutenberg** changed his name in reference either to his mother's surname or the town where she was born. Initially financed by the goldsmith **Johann Fust (?-1466)** (who later sued to recover his investment), Gutenberg introduced to Europe a practical means of using **movable type,** or letters, to print *multiple copies* of documents.

During the 5000 years from the time that alphabets had first been used until the middle of the fifteenth century, every written document created anywhere in the world—with the exception of a few in China—were originals. If multiple examples of an original manuscript were required, they had to be copied by hand, a painstaking task that could take years. In Europe during the **Middle Ages,** Christian monks often devoted their entire lifetimes to making multiple copies of the Bible and other important documents.

Printing—the process of using mechanization to produce multiple copies of a written document—began with the idea of carving blocks to represent letters or words, inking them and then imprinting their images on paper. In 1041, **Bi Zheng (Pi Cheng)** in China was the first to print documents using letters, which he had baked in clay and then formed into sentences. As European trade with China expanded, the printing process became known in the West. In 1423, **Laurence Janszoon Coster (1370-1440)** of Holland experimented with printing in the Roman alphabet using metal characters to produce a clay printing plate. Although these methods were a great improvement over hand-copying, they were still unwieldy.

In 1436, Gutenberg began work on the printing press, a machine that made printing a much faster and more economical procedure. He adapted, or reinvented, Bi Zheng's idea of movable type; that is, the idea of hundreds of individual letters that could be combined in numerous ways to lay out an entire page. Gutenberg published the first mass-produced edition of the Bible—the so-called "42-line Bible" with 42 lines per column—in Mainz in 1456. Within a few decades, there were presses in operation all over Europe. By 1465, the man who had spent his early years dodging lawsuits was awarded high honors for his work by Archbishop Adolf of Mainz.

Although Gutenberg did not invent printing, his work led to the printing press, a machine that launched the greatest revolution in the history of human communications and had a more far-reaching effect than anything that would occur in the next 500 years.

Johann Gutenberg.

Christopher Columbus, the first to prove the widely held belief that the world was indeed spherical in shape and believed that one could travel east or west and eventually return to the same starting point. He was born in Genoa, a port city in Italy, where he grew up around ships and sailors. At that time, European trade with the Far East, which was principally carried on by Venetian traders who followed the route first discovered by **Marco Polo** (see page 39), was flourishing, but Polo's overland route was extremely long and difficult.

Navigators, like Columbus, who believed in the spherical world theory, were convinced they could reach the Far *East* by sailing *west*. Today, we know that the world is a sphere with major land masses in the eastern and western hemispheres. Until the time of Columbus, however, the accepted view in Europe was that the world was flat like a plate, and that if you sailed far enough out on the ocean, you would fall off the edge.

Columbus was willing to undertake the potentially lethal experiment of sailing west to reach the east, and went in search of a government that would underwrite the cost of his adventure. He was turned down by the governments of the Italian city-states of Genoa and Venice, as well as Portugal. He next turned to **King Ferdinand V (1452-1516)** and **Queen Isabella (1451-1501)** of Castille in Spain, who agreed to commit three ships—the *Nina, Pinta* and *Santa Maria*—and crews to the task. Columbus set sail on September 6, 1492 and, after a five-week voyage during which his sailors almost mutinied, the expedition made landfall at San Salvador in the West Indies on October 12.

Few events in the history of humankind have been so momentous as the arrival of Christopher Columbus in the Americas. Columbus did not "discover" America—

Christopher Columbus.

there were up to nine million native people in the Western Hemisphere when he set foot upon the shore at San Salvador. However, Native Americans had no knowledge of the existence of an Eastern Hemisphere any more than the Europeans realized that the Americas existed. The two hemispheres were as different and independent as if they had actually existed on separate planets. What Columbus did was to bring them *together.*

Columbus returned to Spain on March 15, 1493 and made subsequent voyages of colonization in 1493, 1500 and 1502. Columbus died in 1506, still believing that he had reached Asia. His discoveries were treated with enthusiasm by the Spanish authorities, who energetically undertook an exploration and colonization effort that would ultimately lead to a survey of most of the Western Hemisphere's eastern coast within a generation, and the realization that Columbus had in fact discovered a "New World."

The **Renaissance** was an unimaginably brilliant beacon on the highway of history during which a dizzying profusion of exceptional scientists, philosophers and artists simultaneously appeared on the scene in Europe and created works that are still considered extraordinary today. In describing the greatest of these people, later scholars coined the term **Renaissance Man** to denote an individual whose remarkable talents encompassed a variety of fields. There is probably no person who better fits this definition than the illegitimate son of a notary in the small Italian village of Vinci.

One of the greatest geniuses known to history, **Leonardo da Vinci** was an expert in engineering, architecture, biology and botany. His countless accomplishments include pioneering work in the field of human anatomy, the invention of the helicopter and the creation of the world's most famous painting, the *Mona Lisa*.

Apprenticed to the noted painter **Andrea del Verrocchio (1435-1488)** at age 8, da Vinci became a painter at the court of

Leonardo da Vinci.

Lorenzo di Medici (1449-1492) in Florence at 25. He later went to Milan where he created a statue of a horseman for Ludovico Sforza, that at the time was considered to be the greatest work of sculpture in the world. Completed in 1493, it was destroyed in 1500 when the French defeated Sforza. His greatest surviving works of art are a depiction of *The Last Supper* of Jesus Christ and his disciples, which he painted between 1497 and 1501 as a fresco at Turin, and the *Mona Lisa,* a haunting portrait of **Lisa Gioconda (1478-1509?),** a young Tuscan woman, which he completed in 1505. After working in Rome, he went to Amboise in France in 1508. Nothing is known of the life of Lisa Gioconda after 1509, but da Vinci kept her portrait in his possession until his death at Amboise.

More than simply a gifted artist, da Vinci was also a brilliant engineer. He studied the flight of birds and designed parachutes and several flying machines. (With a proper power plant, his helicopter would have worked.) He analyzed the mechanics of the human body and compiled an atlas of its muscles, bones and organs. He was also a pioneer in the study of light and lenses. He designed underwater breathing systems and hydraulic motors. He wrote about geology and the dynamics of rivers, and he designed advanced flood control systems. Despite his lack of formal education in science, da Vinci's work in astronomy, as well as anatomy and engineering, was far ahead of his time. Indeed, his most complex designs were little understood in the sixteenth century.

Da Vinci accomplished so much. He created not only great art, but a virtual library of science from his own outstanding mind. In terms of the importance and breadth of his accomplishments, he may well be regarded as the greatest genius of all time—a true Renaissance man.

The witty Dutch scholar **Desiderius Erasmus** was one of the world's first best-selling authors, earning this distinction during the **Renaissance,** a time of the incredible awakening of art, thought and literature that pulled Europe from the intellectual darkness of the **Middle Ages.** While the Renaissance found many people rediscovering classical Greek and Roman literature and reconsidering classical thought, the true heart of the Renaissance involved a great deal of innovation and invention. Universities sprang up throughout Europe, and there was a great surge in the dissemination of ideas which became possible after Gutenberg's printing press appeared in 1450 and the publishing industry was born.

Desiderius Erasmus.

Born in Rotterdam, Erasmus' **humanist** ideas epitomized the broad-minded, forward thinking of the Renaissance. He studied in the Netherlands and Paris before traveling to England in 1498 to study Greek at Oxford University. His first theological treatise, *The Handbook of the Christian Soldier,* was published in 1503 before he traveled to Venice and Rome, where he was received into the papal circle of **Pope Julius II.**

Erasmus returned to England and became a favorite at the court of **King Henry VIII (1491-1547).** He continued to live in England for nearly a decade before return-ing to the continent in 1517, settling first in Louvain and then Basel, France.

Erasmus' writings were immensely popular because of his clever and amusing insight and his clear, descriptive style, although he attracted numerous highly placed enemies because of his satires. Among his important works are *In Praise of Folly* (1509), in which "folly" speaks to an imaginary audience composed of many types of people; *De Duplici Copia Verborum et Rerum* (1511), a rhetoric textbook for Latin scholars; *Christian Fathers* (1521); *Familiar Colloquies* (1516-1536); *Diatribe de Libero Arbitrio* (1526), a satiric lampoon of Martin Luther; *The Sailings of Ancients* (1532), a series of moral short stories; and *Preparation for Death* (1533). Through his native intellect, his engaging manner and the timely availability of the printing press, Erasmus became the founding father of popular literature.

The first astronomer to depart from the idea that the Earth was the center of the universe, **Nicholas Copernicus** risked charges of heresy to demonstrate mathematically that the Earth rotates around the Sun. Previous astronomers, including **Ptolemy (100-170 AD),** had correctly theorized that the planets and stars were distant celestial bodies rather than gods or magical beasts, but conventional wisdom had held that the Earth, being the most important place in the universe, had to be at its center.

Born at Thorn in Poland, Copernicus studied at the University of Kracow and at Padua and Bologna, Italy. In 1499, he was appointed a professor of mathematics in Rome. He later became a priest, but continued his studies in astronomy, and in 1507 he began working on a treatise, *De Revolutionibus Orbium Celestium,* which he finished in 1530, although it was not actually published until the year he died.

Even though Copernicus incorrectly assumed that all the orbits of the planets were perfectly circular, he was able to demonstrate that the Sun was the focal point of the orbits of the Earth and the other planets and that the Moon alone revolved around the Earth. As a corollary, he also correctly concluded that the Earth rotates upon its own axis, although since the

Nicholas Copernicus.

atmosphere rotates in unison with the Earth's solid surface, there is no apparent movement of the rotation except for the fact the Sun appears to rise and set.

Copernicus' theories were the foundation upon which **Galileo Galilei** (see page 49) and **Sir Isaac Newton** (see page 52) would later build the structure of modern astronomy and of our understanding of the universe.

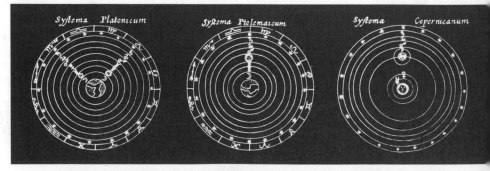

Before Copernicus, astronomers believed that the Sun orbited the Earth.

Generally considered to have been the greatest sculptor of the human form during the **Renaissance**—and perhaps in the entire history of art—**Michaelangelo Buonarroti** (Boo-nə-roo′tē) symbolized the revival of celebrating the magnificence of the human form. His work typified a reawakening of interest in the beauty of natural forms that blossomed during the Renaissance.

Born in Caprese, Italy, Michaelangelo grew up in Florence, where he was surrounded by many of the greatest artists of the time. He studied art and was commissioned as a sculptor by **Lorenzo de Medici (1449-1492),** for whom he created many of his early works. He went to Rome in 1496, and it was here that he created his *Pieta,* a profoundly moving marble portrait of the Madonna cradling the dead Christ in her lap. Upon his return to Florence in 1501, he carved the powerful and monumental *David.* These two works, and *Moses,* which he carved for the tomb of Pope Julius II, are considered to be his greatest sculptures.

Ironically, for a man whose name is almost synonymous with sculpture, Michaelangelo's greatest artistic accomplishment was a series of paintings in the **Sistine Chapel** at the Vatican in Rome, which he executed between 1508 and 1512. While working from a rickety scaffold, he painted over 5800 square feet of the chapel, most of it on the ceiling. In his book, *History of Art,* H.W. Janson described this masterpiece as a "huge organism with hundreds of figures rhythmically distributed." The form and texture of the paintings is so perfect that the sculptor's hand is clearly evident. The subject of the paintings, which are divided into eight major components by meticulously painted architectural details, is the *Story of the Creation.* The most memorable scene is the oft-reproduced *Creation of Adam* in which God's finger touches that of Adam.

After completing the Sistine Chapel, Michaelangelo turned to a series of commissions for the de Medici family, of which two members—Giovanni and Giulio—later became popes. In completing the de Medici projects, which encompassed a chapel, library and mausoleum, he was able to combine sculpture with architecture. In his final years, the great artist immersed himself in architecture and helped to design the magnificent **St. Peter's Basilica,** the centerpiece of the Vatican, which became a focal point for worldwide Christendom and remains so today.

Michaelangelo's *Moses.*

By the end of the fifteenth century, a growing minority of people had come to believe that the Earth was spherical like a globe rather than flat like a plate. The Italian navigator **Christopher Columbus** (see page 41) sought to prove this theory by sailing west to reach the east, and in the process discovered a hemisphere previously unknown to Europeans. Three decades after Columbus completed his voyage of discovery, another adventurer, sailing under the Spanish flag, launched the expedition that eventually proved that the world was indeed a sphere.

Ferdinand Magellan was born **Fernao Magalhães** in Sabrosa, Portugal, and served his king ably as a sailor and sea captain. By the dawn of the sixteenth century, it was clear that although Columbus had found a new continent, he had failed to find a western route to the East Indies. Magellan tried, but failed, to interest the Portuguese government in financing a voyage to accomplish what Columbus had not, so he offered his idea and his services to Charles V of Spain, who accepted.

On September 20, 1519, Magellan set sail from Spain with five ships. Since no one had found a route through the center of the Western Hemisphere, he decided to sail around its southern edge. He traveled southwest and reached landfall near present-day Buenos Aires, Argentina, by mid-October. He followed the coast line south and discovered a passage—albeit a cold and rugged 360-mile trip—around the tip of South America on October 21. This passage, which connects the Atlantic and Pacific Oceans, ever afterward was known as the **Straits of Magellan,** one of the roughest stretches of water on Earth.

When Magellan emerged from the straits, he dubbed the relatively peaceful waters he encountered the "Pacific" Ocean. Sailing across the long, open stretches of the Pacific Ocean left the sailors short of food, and they landed in the **Marianas Islands** to take supplies aboard. The expedition arrived in the **Philippines** in April 1521, where Magellan himself was killed in a fight with the natives on April 27.

Magellan had succeeded in reaching the East Indies by sailing west, and although he died, his crew continued the voyage west to Spain, becoming the first expedition to circumnavigate, or sail completely around, the world. The story of this feat was told by **Antonio Pigafetta,** one of the Magellan's sailors, in his book *The Voyage 'Round the World by Magellan.*

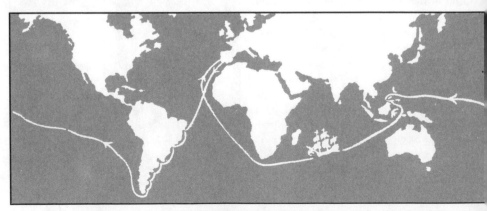

This map shows the course of Magellan's expedition circumnavigating the globe.

40. MARTIN LUTHER
1483-1546

Martin Luther, the man who launched the **Protestant Reformation,** a movement aimed at making fundamental changes in the Roman Catholic Church, was a miner's son born into a pious family at Eisleben in Saxony in eastern Germany. After studying philosophy and classical literature at the University of Efurt, he joined the Augustinian order of monks. In 1507, he was ordained a priest and became a professor of philosophy and theology at Wittenberg the following year.

By Luther's time, the Roman Church had gradually come to wield political as well as spiritual power, filling the void left by the collapse of the Western Roman Empire. Political power often breeds corruption, and so it was with the Church. Despite the presence of many pious and intellectually distinguished churchmen, there were widespread abuses, not the least of which was the selling of **indulgences**—when a believer was promised that payment of money to the Church would allow him to escape the wrath of God's judgment in the afterlife.

Luther was aware that honorable religious men, such as **John Wycliffe (1320-1384)** in England and **John (Jan) Huss (1374-1415)** in Prague, began to speak out against corrupt Church practices, and a growing undercurrent of discontent emerged within the Church itself. Gradually, Luther became determined to take action. On October 31, 1517, he posted a document on the door of the castle church in Wittenberg. This letter, entitled *The 95 Theses Against the Abuse of Indulgences,* accused Archbishop Albrecht of Mainz of fraud in the sale of indulgences. (He was alleged to have pocketed the money.) Luther also condemned the practice of selling indulgences in general.

After Luther's actions attracted a great deal of support, Pope **Leo X (1475-1521)**

Luther posting his letter to the church door.

demanded that he retract what he had said. When Luther refused, he was charged with **heresy** (adhering to a set of beliefs or opinions contrary to official Church teaching), and in 1521 he was **excommunicated** (deprived of his membership in the Church). Nevertheless, many others, especially in Germany, followed his lead and broke away from the Church. They were called Protestants because of their general protest against the Roman Church.

Luther himself organized a new religious movement that embraced the teachings of Christianity but rejected the political authority of the pope in Rome. Luther lived the rest of his life in Eisleben, where he established a school and devoted himself to a German translation of the Bible and other writings. While eventually many Protestant groups came to exist, those who followed Luther's interpretation of Christianity called themselves **Lutherans.**

Today, **Lutheranism** is the dominant religion in Scandinavia, much of Germany and parts of midwestern North America. The revolution launched by Martin Luther did not destroy the Roman Church but actually may have saved it. By forcing Church officials to confront shortcomings in the Church, Luther not only created an alternative form of Christianity but compelled Rome to curb its political abuses.

The most prominent English king since **William the Conqueror** (see page 36) and probably the most controversial, **Henry VIII** was born at Greenwich, the second son of **Henry VII (1457-1509)**, the first English monarch of the **House of Tudor.** Henry came to power during a time of extreme conflict between England and France but was able to make peace between the two nations, even arranging for his sister to marry the French king **Louis XII (1462-1515)**. He assumed the throne in 1509 and that same year married **Catherine of Aragon (1485-1536)**, the widow of his brother Arthur.

After 20 years of marriage with no male heir, Henry wished to terminate his marriage to Catherine, but was refused permission by Pope **Clement VII** because the Catholic Church did not permit divorce. In 1533, Henry's friend, **Thomas Cranmer (1489-1556)**, became Archbishop of Canterbury, the highest church office in England, and the two men worked out an agreement to annul Henry's marriage by having Parliament declare that the **Divine Right of Kings** superseded the authority of the pope. In 1533, Cranmer and Henry withdrew the English wing of the Church from Catholicism and created the **Church of England.**

Later that year, after Henry's marriage to Catherine was annulled, he promptly married **Anne Boleyn (1507-1536)**, with whom he had become enamored but who had refused his advances outside legal marriage. She reigned as his queen for three years and bore him a daughter, **Elizabeth I (1533-1603)**, who later became one of England's most renowned monarchs. When Henry grew tired of Anne, he accused her of adultery and beheaded her on May 19, 1536. He then married **Jane Seymour (1509-1537)**, who died shortly after the birth of their son, **Edward VI (1537-1553)**.

In 1540, in order to create a political alliance with the Protestant princes of northern Germany, Henry married **Anne of Cleves (1515-1557)**, the homely daughter of a German prince, but their marriage lasted less than a year. Henry then married **Catherine Howard (1521-1542)**, the daughter of the Duke of Norfolk, but, like Anne Boleyn before her, Catherine was beheaded for her alleged "immorality." Henry's sixth, and last, wife was **Catherine Parr (1512-1548)**, the daughter of Sir Thomas Parr. A staunch Protestant, she fully supported Henry's still controversial break with the Catholic Church. Catherine outlived Henry by five years.

His inclination for disposing of unwanted spouses aside, Henry is remembered for creating the Church of England, the second major Protestant faith after **Lutheranism,** which was founded by **Martin Luther** (see page 47). He is also known for incorporating **Wales** into the British realm and giving it representation in the English Parliament.

Henry VIII.

The first astronomer to make consistent, systematic use of a telescope, **Galileo Galilei** ushered in a new era in the history of astronomy. Born in Pisa, Italy, the son of mathematician **Vincenzo Galilei,** he was a student of physics in his teens and wrote a treatise on the specific gravity of solid bodies. At 24, he became a professor of mathematics at Pisa. It was here that he postulated the theory that objects of differing weights fall at the same speed and proved it through a now-famous demonstration from the top of the Leaning Tower of Pisa, in which he dropped a metal ball and a wooden ball at the same time. They hit the ground simultaneously.

Between 1592 and 1610, Galileo was a professor at the University of Padua, and in 1609 he built a telescope based on one recently invented by **Hans Lippershey (1570-1619)** in the Netherlands. Turning his telescope to the sky, Galileo saw things no one had ever seen before. On January 7, 1610, he discovered **Io, Europa, Ganymede** and **Callisto,** the four great moons of the planet **Jupiter,** three of which are larger in size than the Earth's Moon.

Galileo Galilei.

Galileo was also able to confirm that Jupiter, in addition to **Mars** and **Venus,** was a spherical body, but the planet **Saturn** confused him. He observed what appeared to be two moons on either side of the planet that never changed position. What he was actually seeing were the edges of Saturn's great ring system. With his telescope, Galileo was able to see the rings, but his instrument was not powerful enough to determine exactly what they were. He studied the surface of the Moon and discovered **sunspots** on the surface of the Sun, which helped prove that it rotated on an axis.

Galileo agreed with, and publicly defended, the theory postulated by **Nicholas Copernicus** (see page 44) that the Sun, not the Earth, was the center of our solar system. In 1616, the Catholic Church, which held the opposite view, forbade Galileo to teach or publish his ideas. Nevertheless, he published his *Dialogue on the Two Principle World Systems* in 1632, incurring the wrath of the Church. Placed under virtual house arrest, Galileo lived the rest of his life near Florence, studying the heavens.

On January 8, 1642, he died, nearly blind from observing sunspots with unprotected eyes. Three hundred and fifty years later—on October 31, 1992—his theories were formally acknowledged by Pope John Paul II.

43. WILLIAM SHAKESPEARE
1564-1616

Amazingly, the best-selling poet and playwright in the world today has been dead for nearly four centuries! **William Shakespeare,** the single greatest figure in the history of English literature, was born at Stratford-upon-Avon on April 23, 1564, the eldest son of glove maker and town politician **John Shakespeare** and **Mary Aden Shakespeare.**

While growing up, Shakespeare enjoyed academic studies as well as sports, especially archery and falconry. In 1582, he married **Anne Hathaway (1557-1623),** and their daughter **Susanna** was born in 1583. Soon after, he relocated his family to London, where he became a successful actor and began to try his hand at writing plays. Despite being an outsider to London's inner circle of writers, his works quickly became popular with actors and audiences alike. Although his plays are undated, his early period in the late 1580s likely included such well-remembered works as *The Comedy of Errors* and *Richard III.* Also in the 1588-1592 period, he took up poetry and produced a number of now famous sonnets.

Between 1594 and 1603, while he was in his thirties, Shakespeare wrote 11 of his most famous comedies, including *Two Gentlemen of Verona, The Taming of the Shrew, A Midsummer Night's Dream, The Merchant of Venice, Much Ado About Nothing, As You Like It* and *Twelfth Night.* Not all of his work during this period consisted of comedies. He also wrote tragedies and historical plays, among which are three of his greatest works: *Henry V, Julius Caesar,* and perhaps the greatest tragic love story in history, *Romeo and Juliet.*

In 1599, the eminently successful Shakespeare and several colleagues involved in the London theater scene built the **Globe Theatre,** then the largest theater in England. It was also about this time that

William Shakespeare is still the world's best-selling playwright.

Shakespeare wrote his greatest drama, *Hamlet, Prince of Denmark.* Soon after, he wrote a series of well-known tragedies: *Othello, King Lear* and *Antony and Cleopatra.*

In 1610, Shakespeare retired to Stratford, where he continued to both write independently and collaborate with other writers. The last play that he wrote entirely by himself before his death on April 23, 1616 was *The Tempest.*

Today, many of his works have become an integral part of the high school and college curriculums in English-speaking (and many other) nations. Not only are his plays continuously in production throughout the world, but theater companies—both in small towns such as Ashland, Oregon, and major metropolitan cities, such as London—specialize in presenting his plays.

England's only non-royal rulers in the past 1200 years were **Oliver Cromwell** and his son, **Richard (1626-1712)**. Born at Huntingdon of Welsh descent, Oliver Cromwell was a descendent of the Williams clan and adopted the name Cromwell in deference to **Thomas Cromwell,** whose agent he was in the suppression of monasteries. A stern, straightlaced **Puritan** who was outspoken in his antagonism to religious absolutism, he became a member of Parliament and served as a cavalry officer for the Parliamentary forces in the English Civil War.

The English ruling **House of Stuart,** which began with the reign of **James I (1566-1625)** in 1603, was far more authoritarian than the preceding House of Tudor, and relations with Parliament were strained. After **Charles I (1600-1649)** succeeded James in 1625, the political situation further deteriorated. Charles carried on a running battle with Scotland and increased taxes, and by 1642, the ongoing Stuart estrangement with Parliament turned into open civil war.

Cromwell, leading the Parliamentary forces, won decisive victories at Marston Moor in 1644 and at Maseby in 1645. Charles surrendered and was subsequently executed in 1649. Parliament then continued to rule England with a Council of State until 1653, when Cromwell was named **Protector.** As such, he was the first non-monarch to rule England in the 825 years since the Saxon King **Egbert (775-839 AD)** had first occupied the throne in 828 AD.

Although Cromwell's aptitude for leading troops in battle made him a strong leader, he proved to be just as authoritarian as the Stuarts, and thus he made many enemies. Consolidating his power, he dissolved Parliament and ruled England militarily. Although he presided over a prosperous time in England's economic history, a groundswell of public opinion arose to support a restoration of the monarchy.

When Cromwell died in 1658, his son, Richard was named **Lord Protector,** but he lacked the resolve to continue his father's rule. After his resignation in 1659, he was succeeded in 1660 by a restoration of the House of Stuart in the person of **Charles II (1630-1685).**

Although Oliver Cromwell is remembered today as either a hero or villain, he remains a singularly unique figure who shaped the course of English history during one of its most turbulent times.

Oliver Cromwell.

45. SIR ISAAC NEWTON
1642-1727

Born in England at Woolsthorpe, Lincolnshire, and educated at Trinity College, Cambridge, **Isaac Newton** was one of the greatest scientific geniuses in the history of the world. He was certainly the greatest European scientist who lived between the time of Archimedes and that of Albert Einstein. Before he was 24, he had invented the **binomial theorem** and **functional calculus,** discovered the **spectrum of light** and had written his **Theory of Gravitation.** The latter allegedly occurred to him while he was watching an apple fall from a tree in 1665.

Newton also invented the **reflector telescope,** which differed from the simpler **refractor type** invented by **Hans Lippershey (1570-1619)** in 1608. In the reflector type, the light was not simply magnified but reflected directly to the eye from a large, concave mirror via a small, flat mirror, without passing through glass.

In 1667, when he was 25, Newton was elected a fellow at Trinity College. It was while he was at Cambridge that he developed his **Three Laws of Motion,** the monumental achievement of a young life that had already experienced several major milestones.

The Three Laws were:

1. **Inertia:** Every body, if left to itself, free of action of other bodies, will remain at rest if it is at rest, or it will continue to move at constant velocity if it is in motion.
2. **Motion:** The rate of change of the momentum of a body measures, in direction and magnitude, the force acting on it.
3. **Reaction:** For every action there is an equal and opposite reaction.

In 1687, he published his *Mathematical Principles of Natural Philosophy.* In this work, known universally as the *Principia* (because it was written and originally pub-

Sir Isaac Newton.

lished in Latin) Newton demonstrated the structure of the universe, the movement of the planets and calculated the mass of the Sun, the planets and their moons. Where Columbus and Magellan had proven that the Earth was spherical, Newton proved that the Earth is *not* a perfect sphere but rather an *oblate spheroid*—slightly flattened at the poles by the centrifugal force of its own rotation. His theoretical work with light and telescopes was combined into a single compendium entitled *Optics* which was published in 1704.

Newton served in the English Parliament from 1701 to 1705, was knighted by Queen Anne in 1705, and served as president of the Royal Society from 1703 until his death at Kensington in 1727.

Just as Marco Polo and Christopher Columbus expanded our ancestors' view of the geographical parameters of the world, Newton did more than anyone before to help people understand the physical forces that govern all matter, from the stars in the sky to the apples on a backyard tree.

The father of modern classical music and one of the most prolific geniuses in the history of Western music, **Johann Sebastian Bach** was born in Eisenach, Germany, the son of the town musician and part of a family whose professional musical heritage spanned over 100 years. He spent his entire life in Germany, writing, teaching and performing music. Orphaned at age 10, he went to live with his brother **Johann Christoph Bach,** an organist in nearby Ohrdruf. After completing his musical studies, in 1703 he secured an appointment as an organist for the church in Arnstadt. Two years later, he attended a concert in Lubeck given by organist **Dietrich Buxtehude (1637-1707),** who became a great influence on his later life and career.

Johann Sebastian Bach.

In 1717, after nine years as a court organist at Weimar, Bach spent six years as the court conductor for **Prince Leopold of Anhalt-Cöthen.** It was here that he had the opportunity to write some of the works by which his reputation is sustained today. His six **Brandenburg Concertos** for chamber orchestra are among the leading masterpieces of classical music.

Bach's first wife, **Maria Barbara Bach,** died in 1720, having borne him seven children. In 1721, he married **Anna Magdalena Wilckin,** a gifted singer for whom he had written several vocal scores. Over the ensuing years, the couple had 13 children. Raised in a musical household, four of their sons later became well-regarded composers. They were **Wilhelm Friedemann Bach (1710-1784), Karl Philipp Emanuel Bach (1714-1788), Johann Christoph Friedrich Bach (1732-1775)** and **Johann Christian Bach (1735-1782).**

In 1723, Bach accepted a post at the **Thomas Schule (School)** in Leipzig and remained there for the rest of his life. The constant need for new compositions allowed him to flourish in his role as composer, and he produced an amazing number of cantatas, fugues, chorales and other compositions. A virtuoso at the organ, he was able to compose and improvise brilliantly intricate works. A master in the use of counterpoint, his music opened up a whole new vista not only for the organ, but for the violin, harpsichord and other orchestral instruments as well.

The organ was Bach's instrument of choice.

The most important figure in classical French literature, **Voltaire** was to the written word what **Leonardo da Vinci** (see page 42) was to art and engineering. He wrote both fiction and nonfiction in a witty, yet polished, style. He was also a well-regarded philosopher and scientist, who had studied with **Sir Isaac Newton** (see page 52) and taught literature to **Frederick the Great** (see page 56).

Born in Paris to a respectable middle-class family, Voltaire was well-read and a writer of poetry. His satire delighted many but enraged those in official academic circles. To escape harassment in France, he traveled to England in 1762, where he befriended, and was influenced by, poet **Alexander Pope (1688-1744)**, poet and satirist **Jonathan Swift (1667-1745)**, and philosopher **John Locke (1632-1704)**. He became fluent in English, and upon his return to Paris in 1729, he introduced his countrymen to the works of **William Shakespeare** (see page 50). By this time, his literary career had begun to thrive, and his fiction, such as *La Henride* (1730) and *Zaire* (1732), became popular. His satiric *Philosophical Letters* (1734) incurred the wrath of the academic establishment which he had attacked.

Between 1734 and 1749, Voltaire traveled throughout Europe, but spent most of his time with **Emilie du Chatelet (1706-1749),** a mathematician and Newtonian scientist, at a laboratory they had built in Cirey. In 1738, his *Elements of Newton's Philosophy* was published in Holland, where he became friends with Frederick the Great. After du Chatelet's death, Voltaire accepted Frederick's invitation to come to his court at Potsdam, where he became the emperor's literary mentor. After the two men had a falling out, Voltaire retired to Les Delices, his home near Geneva. It was here that he wrote *Candide* (1759), one his greatest works of fiction, and many other historical and philosophical works, including *The Philosophical Dictionary* (1764).

In 1778, his return to Paris was such a cause for celebration among his followers that the prolonged festivities wore him down to the point of exhaustion, a contributing factor to his death. A very popular writer in his time, he is remembered today as being the first great French historian and the most highly regarded writer in that language.

Voltaire.

The birth of the United States as a nation was attended by an uncommonly large group of outstanding statesmen. Among these, one of the most gifted, was diplomat, writer and inventor **Benjamin Franklin.**

Born in Boston, Massachusetts, on January 17, 1706, Franklin left home at age 17 and became an apprentice printer in Philadelphia. Pennsylvania governor William Keith promised to financially back him in his own print shop, but withdrew his support while Franklin was in England buying type. Staying on in England, Franklin worked in various print shops until he was able to save enough money to return home and open his own shop in 1726. His business flourished, and two years later he began publishing the *Pennsylvania Gazette,* one of the most influential newspapers of the era. In 1731, he founded what was probably the first public library in America. In 1732, he began writing and publishing *Poor Richard's Almanack,* an annual collection of stories and insights about life, love, politics and other human activities. In 1747, he began experiments in support of the hypothesis that lightning was an electrical phenomenon, which culminated with his invention of the **lightning rod.**

Franklin served as a clerk, and later Assemblyman, in the Pennsylvania General Assembly from 1736 to 1757. He traveled to England, where he was well received by members of the literary and scientific community, who respected his work. After returning to Philadelphia in 1762, he was again elected to the Assembly.

Franklin strongly endorsed the generally held view that Britain should relax its control over the American colonies and allow colonists a larger governing role in their own affairs. In 1774, he went to England to present a petition to King **George III (1738-1820)** on behalf of the colonists and

Benjamin Franklin.

the newly formed **Continental Congress.** The king and the House of Lords rejected his petition, and by the time Franklin returned to Philadelphia, the **American Revolutionary War (1775-1783)** had already begun.

After his election to the **Second Continental Congress,** Franklin organized the postal system, became postmaster general and helped **Thomas Jefferson** (see page 59) write the **Declaration of Independence,** which was signed on July 4, 1776. In 1776, Franklin was appointed as the American ambassador to France, and while serving in this capacity, he was able to convince the French government to support the American cause with both arms and supplies.

After the war, Franklin helped negotiate the peace treaty with Britain in 1782-1783. He returned to the United States from France in 1785 and became a member of the **Constitutional Convention** in 1787. Upon his death on April 17, 1790, Franklin was eulogized from Virginia to Boston to Paris, and his funeral in Philadelphia attracted a record number of mourners.

The son of the Prussian king **Frederick Wilhelm I (1688-1740)** and grandson of **Frederick I (1657-1713)**, **Frederick II** is remembered as perhaps the greatest monarch in German history. Born in Berlin and physically abused by his father, he grew up determined to achieve greatness that exceeded that of his forebears.

Frederick succeeded his father to the throne on May 31, 1740, and in October of that year, Charles VI of Austria died and was succeeded by his daughter, **Maria Theresa (1717-1780).** Frederick seized the opportunity to claim Silesia, and in an armed confrontation with Austria, captured it. While Maria Theresa was occupied with the **War of Austrian Succession (1740-1748),** Frederick invaded Bohemia and Saxony, bringing them within the Prussian sphere of influence.

In 1756, when Frederick learned that Austria had formed a secret alliance with France and Russia, he allied himself with Britain's **George II (1683-1760).** Together they defeated Austria, then France, in the **Seven Years War (1756-1763),** which was played out in North America as the **French & Indian War.** The **Treaty of Hurbertsburg,** signed on February 15, 1763, allowed Prussia to retain its conquered territory, making it the pre-eminent German state. In 1772, along with **Catherine the Great (1729-1796)** of Russia, he engineered the **First Partition of Poland,** which allowed him to obtain West Prussia and prevent Austria from acquiring Bavaria.

During the remainder of his rule, Frederick focused much of his energy on reorganizing the Prussian government. Characterized by historians as an "enlightened absolutist," he greatly revised and modernized the judiciary and issued a new codification of Prussian law, the *Codex Fredericanus.*

Frederick II.

His reorganization of the officer corps of the Prussian army created a caste of intensely disciplined, well-trained professional officers, whose legacy survived until the twentieth century. He also undertook numerous public works projects, such as canals, roads and bridges. A great admirer of **George Washington** (see page 58), in 1785 he became one of the first European monarchs to conclude a commercial treaty with the United States.

Born in Maton, Yorkshire, England, **James Cook** was perhaps the greatest of the English sea captains and one of the greatest explorers of the epoch of world discovery that began with **Christopher Columbus** (see page 41). Cook learned his trade while working on commercial ships that plied the waters of the North and Baltic Seas, and in 1755, at the age of 27, he took command of his first Royal Navy ship. Assigned to North America, he surveyed the St. Lawrence River and the coast of Newfoundland. Having proven himself to be a navigational genius, he was given command of a 1768 expedition to take English astronomers to view a transit of Venus from the South Pacific. After this, he explored the region for the British crown.

Cook also visited New Zealand, where a group of 15 islands still bear his name, and became the first person to chart its entire coastline. In 1770, he visited New Guinea and claimed the east coast of Australia for England under the name New South Wales. On this first voyage, Cook had explored more of this territory than any other explorer before him. In 1772, Cook set out again, this time to search for the rumored, but as yet uncharted, "Southern Continent." He found it and became the first man to map the coastline of Antarctica. He had sailed 70,000 miles (112,000 km) on this voyage, during which he had become the first person to sail around the Earth from east to west.

On his third voyage in 1776, Cook discovered the Hawaiian Islands, which he named the Sandwich Islands after **John Montagu (1718-1792),** the fourth earl of Sandwich and the first lord of the British Admiralty. Cook in turn explored the North American coast from Oregon to Alaska and sailed through the Bering Strait into the Arctic Ocean. It was in 1779, during this third voyage, that he was stabbed to death in Hawaii. Like **Ferdinand Magellan** (see page 46), he died while on a voyage of exploration.

Cook's greatest legacy was that his explorations paved the way for the settlement of Australia and New Zealand, which had already began before his death, and the fact that he was the first person to explore all the myriad lands within, and on the rim of, the world's largest ocean.

James Cook.

One of history's greatest military leaders, **George Washington** was responsible for the defeat of the British and served as the first president of the newly formed nation of the **United States of America.** Born on February 22, 1732 in Westmoreland County, Virginia, he was a surveyor by trade and a landowner by inheritance, and in 1759 he married **Martha Dandridge Custis (1732-1802).** While serving as an officer in the Virginia Militia during the early years of the **French & Indian War (1754-1763),** he began to develop an animosity for British officers and their troops who generally treated American-born citizens like a subjugated enemy.

Elected to the Virginia House of Burgesses, or Assembly, in 1758, Washington became deeply aware of the growing resentment that a majority of Americans felt about living in a British colony. In 1765, the British Parliament enacted the **Stamp Act,** which levied a tax on colonists to pay for a British military force to occupy the colonies and strengthen the power of the British governors. In 1774, after the British governor of Virginia dissolved the House of Burgesses, Washington was among those who realized that an armed conflict with England had become inevitable, and said so.

As an open rebellion, known as the **American Revolutionary War (1775-1783),** erupted throughout the colonies, Washington distinguished himself as commander of the Virginia militia units, and in 1775, the newly formed **Continental Congress** made him commander of the American army. On July 4, 1776, the American **Declaration of Independence** was signed. Washington was able to successfully force the British out of Boston, but he failed to hold New York City.

On December 24, 1776, he launched a daring and brilliant attack across the

George Washington.

Delaware River and smashed the British defenses at Trenton and Princeton. In terms of American morale, this proved to be the turning point of the war, but the moment of final victory occurred when Washington decisively defeated British general **Lord Charles Cornwallis (1738-1805)** at **Yorktown** on October 19, 1781. Although a peace treaty was not signed until 1783, the British had been vanquished and a new nation was born.

After the war, Washington retired to his home at Mount Vernon in Virginia, but in 1787 he presided over the **Constitutional Convention** in Philadelphia. In 1789, under the provisions of the **United States Constitution,** he was elected by the **Electoral College** as the first president of the United States. Re-elected in 1793, Washington built a strong central government, but one which was governed by consensus of state representatives. One of the most highly regarded statesmen in United States history, he declined a third presidential term and retired in 1797. He died on December 14, 1799.

The third president of the United States, **Thomas Jefferson** is remembered as the primary author of the American **Declaration of Independence** and as the architect of basic American government theory and practice, from the design of its monetary system and its system of weights and measures to the organization of its primary democratic institutions. Born in Albemarle County, Virginia, on April 13, 1743, Jefferson's background and early career were similar to that of **George Washington** (see page 58), and both men served as Virginia state legislators. However, Washington gained national prominence as a leader through his military career, while Jefferson became renowned as a man of great intellect and a legal scholar.

Jefferson graduated from the College of William & Mary and was admitted to the Virginia bar in 1767. He was elected to the Virginia House of Burgesses, or Assembly, in 1769 and won a great deal of respect and attention for his writings on the subject of American independence. While a member of the **Continental Congress,** he drafted the Declaration of Independence in 1776. During the **American Revolutionary War (1775-1783),** he served as governor of Virginia, and in 1784 the Continental Congress chose him as its minister to France.

When Washington was elected president in 1789, Jefferson served as his Secretary of State, often finding himself at odds with the Secretary of the Treasury, **Alexander Hamilton (1757-1784),** who favored a more powerful role for central government, a philosophy which Jefferson viewed as "monarchist in principle." In 1796, Jefferson ran as the Democratic-Republican party candidate for president against Washington's vice-president, **John Adams (1735-1826),** the candidate of the Federalist Party. Adams won, but in a rematch in 1800, Jefferson was elected to his first of two four-year presidential terms. In his first term, Jefferson lowered taxes and cut the federal budget, two measures that helped create widespread prosperity at the beginning of the nineteenth century.

In 1803, in his most memorable act as president, Jefferson struck a deal with **Napoleon Bonaparte** (see page 62) to acquire a vast expanse of French-held land in North America known as **Louisiana.** Controversial at the time, the **Louisiana Purchase** nearly doubled the area of the United States and set the stage for a mass migration of people westward across the North American continent to the Pacific Ocean.

Jefferson retired to Monticello, his home in Virginia, in 1809, where he designed the University of Virginia. He died on July 4, 1826—the same day as John Adams—on the fiftieth anniversary of the signing of the Declaration of Independence.

Thomas Jefferson.

53. WOLFGANG AMADEUS MOZART
1756-1791

Generally recognized as history's foremost musical genius, **Wolfgang Amadeus Mozart** was born in Salzburg, Austria, the son of **Leopold Mozart,** the musician to the Archbishop of Salzburg. Both Wolfgang and his older sister **Marianne** (aka **Nannerl**) were considered musical prodigies at an early age. Indeed, Wolfgang was composing minuets at age five. Their father took the two children to visit the emperor in Vienna, and eventually traveled with them to France and Holland. By the time he was 10, Mozart had composed four symphonies and a popular oratorio, and at age 14 he conducted his opera *Mithridate* from the harpsichord at Milan's **La Scala,** Europe's largest opera house.

Despite his musical brilliance—or perhaps because of it—Mozart failed to obtain a long-term appointment as a court composer, so he spent the years from 1771 to 1787 traveling and writing for commissions throughout Europe: Milan, Vienna, Munich, Augsburg, Mannheim and Paris. In 1778, he fell in love with the beautiful and talented soprano **Aloysia Weber,** the cousin of composer **Karl Maria von Weber (1786-1826).** After she failed to return his affections, he married Aloysia's sister, **Constanze** four years later.

Constanze proved to be just as impractical as her husband, who was as inept at managing his income and his business affairs as he was gifted at writing musical compositions. The latter was extremely easy for him, and he could create entire movements in his head, then write them down later at his leisure, often while engaged in other activities. He was also an excellent conductor and musician, mastering the violin as well as keyboard instruments.

As a composer, Mozart was preeminent in operatic, religious, symphonic and chamber music. In short, he was a genius who possessed an almost unlimited range of musical talent.

In 1786 and 1787, Mozart wrote two of history's greatest operas, *The Marriage of Figaro* and *Don Giovanni.* Also in 1787, Austrian court composer **Christoph Gluck (1714-1787)** died and Mozart was appointed to his position. Over a seven-week span in 1788, Mozart wrote three of his most well-known symphonies, *E Flat, G Minor* and *C* (the *Jupiter*). In 1790, he wrote the operas *Cosi Fan Tutte* and *The Magic Flute,* the latter considered by many not only to be his most memorable opera but the greatest opera ever written in German.

Despite the immense success of Mozart's compositions and the teaching work he did at court, he was unable to successfully manage his money and so lived in poverty. Though he was taken ill and died at the age of 35, Mozart created a greater body of masterful work in his short life than any other composer before or since.

Wolfgang Amadeus Mozart.

Ludwig von Beethoven.

Known as the "Michealangelo of Music" for his great artistic genius and the enormous range of the music he wrote, **Ludwig von Beethoven** was born in the university town of Bonn, Germany, on the Rhine River. His father, **Johann Beethoven,** a second-generation professional musician, made him practice the piano constantly, and by the age of 14 he had achieved a notable reputation. However, after his mother died, his father became an alcoholic and Beethoven went to live with **Madam von Breuning,** whose home was a gathering place for the leading musicians of the day. Here he met composer **Franz Josef Haydn (1732-1809),** who invited him to study in Vienna, then the music capital of Europe.

Between 1792 and 1802, Beethoven wrote a number of works reminiscent of Mozart and Haydn, but after 1803, his own unique talent began to emerge. By 1815, he had written the opera *Fidelio* and several piano sonatas, as well as several of his most well-known symphonies, including the *E Flat Major* (the *Third* or *Eroica*), the *B Flat Major* (*Fourth*), *C Minor* (the *Fifth* or *Fate Symphony*), *F Major* (the *Sixth* or *Pastoral*), *A Major* (*Seventh*) and *F Major* (*Eighth*).

Beethoven's *Eroica* or *Heroic Symphony* was originally dedicated to **Napoleon Bonaparte** (see page 62), whom Beethoven and many others saw as being the "God-sent deliverer of Europe from the decay of the Middle Ages." However, Beethoven later became displeased when Napoleon crowned himself emperor.

By the time of his *Fifth* and *Sixth* symphonies, Beethoven was growing progressively deaf, and his *Fifth Symphony* is seen as symbolic not only of man's struggle with fate but of the composer's own personal struggle with deafness. His *Pastoral Symphony* was written in praise of the rural countryside, where he lived briefly after he canceled his marriage to his "Immortal Beloved One," most likely **Theresa Brunswick,** the sister of Count Franz von Brunswick.

During 1811 and 1812, Beethoven spent a great deal of time with German poet, playwright and author **Johann Wolfgang von Goethe (1749-1832)** and it was Goethe's drama *Egmont* that inspired his *Seventh Symphony* by the same name, considered his most joyful. Beethoven's last symphony, the *Ninth* or *Choral,* which debuted in Vienna in 1824, was inspired by the *Ode to Joy,* a work by classical German poet and author **Johann Christoph Friedrich von Schiller (1759-1805).** By this time, however, the composer of some of the world's most powerful symphonies was almost totally deaf.

Although Beethoven, like Mozart, died an unhappy man, his musical legacy far eclipsed the tragedy of his personal life. Beethoven brought music to the forefront of the cultural and intellectual life of Western society like never before.

55. NAPOLEON BONAPARTE
1769-1821

The greatest leader in the history of France, **Napoleon Bonaparte** was born of Italian ancestry at Ajaccio, Corsica, on August 15, 1769. Educated at military schools in Brienne and Paris, France, Napoleon entered the French Army in 1785 just before the time of the **French Revolution (1789-1799)** and he witnessed the fall of the French monarchy in 1792. He played a role in defeating the English at Toulon in 1793 and was given command of French artillery for the invasion of Italy in 1794. Having won a series of brilliant victories against the Austrians in Italy, Napoleon, now a general, led the invasion of Egypt in 1798, marched into Cairo and then into Jerusalem. These events greatly inspired the French public and Napoleon returned to France as a national hero. Meanwhile, France had been without a single leader for a decade. The weak, ineffective ruling Directoire that ruled France was on the verge of collapse, and in 1799 it was replaced by a **Consulate** with Napoleon as first consul.

Due to Napoleon's immense popularity, the French people—who had thrown out the Bourbon kings in 1792—allowed him to be crowned emperor of the French at Notre Dame Cathedral in Paris on May 18, 1804, and invited the pope to do the honors. However, when the climactic moment came, he lifted the crown from the pope's hands and crowned himself. He felt that no one else was worthy to do it.

Napoleon's dream of a French empire began to take shape. He already controlled France, the Netherlands and Italy, but was opposed by Austria, England, Russia and Prussia. He planned an invasion of England, which he was forced to call off, but he defeated the Russian and Austrian armies at **Austerlitz** in December 1805. He went on to defeat the Prussians at **Jena** in 1806 and the Austrians at **Friedland** in 1807. By this time, Napoleon had accom-

Napoleon Bonaparte.

plished his goal of effectively controlling an area of Europe even larger than Charlemagne's empire. He now dominated France, Poland, Italy and every country in between, including Austria and all the German states of the old Holy Roman Empire.

In 1810, when the Russians refused to join his blockade, he decided to invade Russia. He managed to capture Moscow in September 1812, but after severe winter weather threatened his supply lines, he was forced to retreat. This military disaster was the beginning of the end of Napoleon's reign of power. After Austrian and German states rose up against his rule, he was forced to withdraw and his empire collapsed. On April 11, 1814, he abdicated and was forced into exile on the island of Elba. The man who had once ruled most of Europe was now a tenant on a tiny, rocky island.

The departure of Napoleon in 1814 left France in a state of total chaos not unlike that which it had experienced during the Revolution. Amazingly, at this point the Bourbon monarchy was restored, but Louis XVIII ruled for only 10 months.

Napoleon, having grown increasingly restless during his exile, returned to France. He was welcomed back in Paris with open arms, mostly for nostalgic reasons, as he represented France's past glory. For a brief 100 days beginning on March 10, 1815, the clock seemed to have been turned back a decade.

However, old enemies were not at all pleased that he was back on the throne. Napoleon knew that he must move quickly to restore his empire. He had to gamble that a fast victory would bring the states of Europe toppling like a line of dominoes. A large British/Prussian/Dutch force, under the command of the Prussian General **Gebhart Leberecht von Blücher** (Bloo′kər) **(1742-1819)** and **Arthur Wellesley (1769-1852),** the **Duke of Wellington,** gathered in Belgium. Napoleon's large, well-equipped force drove a wedge between Blücher and Wellington, and defeated the Prussians at **Ligny** on June 16. The British retreated to a little crossroads village called **Waterloo,** where Napoleon caught up with them on June 17. He prepared to attack Wellington on June 18, but rain made it difficult to move his cannons into position. Napoleon finally attacked at 11 a.m. and the battle raged for 10 hours. By the morning of June 19, the French had been defeated and 50,000 men lay dead and dying.

Waterloo was one of the major turning points in European history because if Napoleon had won, he stood a good chance of re-establishing his empire and of once again making France the dominant power in Europe—and possibly the world—for the rest of the nineteenth century.

As it was, France would never regain the power and influence that it had enjoyed under Napoleon. He had lost the French empire in Europe and he had sold an even larger area—**Louisiana**—in North America to the United States. Waterloo marked the beginning of *Pax Britannica,* a period of more than a century during which Britain reigned as the world's leading superpower.

Napoleon himself retreated to Paris, where he abdicated, for the second time, four days later. He surrendered to the British and was taken to the island of St. Helena in the South Atlantic where he lived until his death from cancer on May 8, 1821.

Napoleon's most lasting legacy was not that his conquests had given France a moment of glory. His greatest contribution was his **Code Napoleon,** a modern structure of civil laws that dramatically reshaped the French legal system and influenced the legal systems in the other nations under his rule. The Code Napoleon remains the basis for French law to this day.

Napoleon crowned himself emperor.

The two names of **William Clark** and **Merriwether Lewis** are inextricably linked in our historical memory because of the unprecedented two-year expedition which they undertook that succeeded in surveying more of the North American continent than any previous expedition, and which gave the United States its first sense of its geographic importance. Clark was born in Virginia, the younger brother of the great American Revolutionary War hero **George Rogers Clark (1752-1818),** under whom he served as a lieutenant from 1786-1896. Lewis was also born in Virginia and served under George Clark during the Indian wars of the 1790s.

In 1803, President **Thomas Jefferson** (see page 59) concluded an agreement with **Napoleon Bonaparte** (see page 62) to purchase a vast tract of North American territory owned by France and named for King Louis XIV. The **Louisiana Purchase** nearly doubled the size of the United States, but it was a immense, mysterious place that few men had ever seen. To explore Louisiana, Jefferson chose Lewis, who selected Clark as his co-captain. Together they assembled a group of surveyors, scientists and others and sailed north from St. Louis, Missouri, on the Mississippi River on March 14, 1804. While wintering with the Mandan Indians near present-day Bismarck, North Dakota, they met **Sacajawea (1784?-1812 or 1884),** a Shoshone woman who had been captured by the Mandans. She went on to serve as an interpreter for the expedition and as an emissary to the Shoshone and other western tribes. As such, she was an integral element in the success of the Lewis & Clark Expedition.

During the spring and summer of 1805, Lewis and Clark split up and between them explored much of what is now the state of Montana. They joined up again on August 17 and crossed the **Continental Divide** in

Lewis and Clark with Sacajawea.

the Rocky Mountains, and with the help of the Shoshone, Nez Perce and Flathead Indian tribes, they traveled to the Clearwater River, where they constructed long boats for a trip down the Snake River and ultimately into the great Columbia River.

On November 7, the expedition reached the mouth of the Columbia at the Pacific Ocean. Three months later, they began the difficult journey back up a network of rivers to the Divide. Again, the two men traveled separate routes, meeting at the headwaters of the Missouri River on August 11, 1806. On September 23, they returned to St. Louis. Their scientific and ethnographic report to Washington was a milestone in the documentation of North America's natural history.

Merriwether Lewis was subsequently appointed governor of Louisiana in 1807 but was killed—possibly murdered—in 1809. William Clark went on to serve as the superintendent of Indian affairs for Louisiana (1807-1813), as governor of the Missouri Territory (1813-1821), surveyor general of Illinois, Missouri and Arkansas (1824-1825) and federal superintendent of Indian affairs (1822-1833).

Known simply as "the Liberator," **Simón Bolívar** was to five South American nations what **George Washington** (see page 58) was to the United States. Just as Washington's efforts ended British rule in a large part of North America, so too did Bolívar's activities effectively act as the catalyst that ended Spanish colonial rule in all of South America.

Bolívar was born into the nobility in Venezuela and was educated in Madrid. Even in his student days he took an interest in the increasingly popular movement to free his homeland from Spanish rule. He spent time in England, France and the United States, returning to Venezuela shortly before it declared its independence on July 5, 1811. He became an officer in the army of liberation and in 1813 he captured the capital city of Caracas. Forced out by the royalists, he returned in 1816, achieving total control in 1819. Made dictator of Venezuela, he set out to liberate New Grenada from Spanish rule. Once again victorious, he merged New Grenada with Venezuela, renaming it **Columbia** after **Christopher Columbus** (see page 41). On August 30, 1821, he became president of Columbia.

The following year, Bolívar defeated the Spanish at Pichincha, Ecuador, successfully freeing a third South American state. After two more years of heavy fighting, he drove the Spanish from Peru, and in 1825 he freed Upper Peru, which was renamed **Bolivia** in his honor. In 1826, he created a Bolivian constitution, naming himself "president for life" and turned the government of Peru over to a hand-picked council.

In September 1826, Bolívar returned to Columbia, where he was re-elected president. By this time, many people began to question his motives, fearing he might have become a greedy empire builder not unlike **Napoleon Bonaparte** (see page 62). Although Bolívar assumed total dictatorial power in 1828, the tide of public opinion had turned against him. In November 1829, Venezuela seceded from Columbia and Bolívar, like Napoleon before him, was forced out of office and into retirement.

From a historical perspective, Bolívar can be viewed as a true liberator, for he gained little wealth from his conquests—even spending his own inheritance on his campaigns—and his primary motive throughout his public career was the establishment of republican governments in colonies formerly controlled by Spain.

Simón Bolívar.

65

Samuel Morse, who emerged as the father of modern communications technology, was born at Charlestown, Massachusetts, the son of the Reverend **Jedidiah Morse (1761-1826),** the compiler of the first American geography. Morse graduated from Yale University in 1810 as a well-known portrait painter and later founded and served as the first president (1826-1842) of the **National Academy of Design.** In 1832, he became a professor of painting and sculpture at the University of the City of New York (now New York University). While traveling in France, he met **Louis-Jacques Daguerre (1789-1851),** the inventor of practical photography, and introduced the **daguerreotype** method of photography into the United States.

By the nineteenth century, as the steam engine boosted the speed and distance capabilities of vehicles on both land and sea, a clear need emerged for a means of instantaneous communication over long distances. It became critical to quickly communicate with places that were too far away to be seen visually, just to keep ahead of the faster ships and trains. The idea of sending coded messages by means of electricity dates back to the early eighteenth century. However, it was Morse who developed the first practical **telegraph** system.

Morse conceived the idea while aboard a ship returning from Europe in 1832, and he worked for several years to develop the **electromagnetic relay system** that would eventually make telegraphy practical. Morse first demonstrated his telegraph to President **Martin Van Buren (1782-1862)** on February 21, 1838, and by 1843 a workable commercial telegraph line was in place between Washington and Baltimore. On May 24, 1844, he sent his historic message from the Supreme Court: "What God hath wrought."

Samuel Morse.

Within the next two years, most major American and European cities were connected by telegraph, and in the 1850s, England and Sweden were linked to continental Europe by means of underwater cables. Europe and America were joined by an underwater cable between Newfoundland and Ireland in 1858, and **Queen Victoria (1819-1901)** sent a 90-word message to President **James Buchanan (1791-1868).** The advent of instantaneous long distance communications revolutionized the way people viewed time and distance. Morse also devised the **Morse Code,** which consisted of a series of taps of the key that made electrical contact. Thus each letter of the alphabet consisted of short taps (dots) combined with longer contacts (dashes). This system became the universal "language" of the telegraph and a precursor to the **binary system** used in all modern computers and electronic communications.

The son of English author **Isaac d'Israeli (1766-1848)**, author and statesman **Benjamin Disraeli** was born in London into the Jewish faith but baptized in the Church of England at the age of 13. At 17, he began studying law, but showed a more ardent interest in literature. His

Disraeli as a young man.

first, somewhat biographical, novel *Vivien Grey* (1826) was a best-seller, but his later work was less commercially successful.

In 1837, Disraeli won a seat in the House of Commons as a **Tory** (Conservative) and represented several constituencies Maidstone, Shrewsbury and later Buckinghamshire). In 1845, he succeeded **Sir Robert Peel (1788-1850)** as leader of the his party, a post that he retained for the rest of his life. Disraeli's guiding political philosophy was his belief that England could be a great nation only through a synthesis of tradition with democracy, and that the best interest of the average Briton was served by maintaining the established roles of church and state.

Disraeli served as chancellor of the Exchequer (equivalent to the American secretary of the treasury) in 1852, 1858-1859 and 1866 and as prime minister in 1868 and 1874-1880. Among his many achievements was the **Reform Bill of 1867,** which redistributed Parliamentary seats and greatly increased the number of voters. In 1875, he directed Britain's purchase of a controlling interest in the six-year-old **Suez Canal,** a manmade channel built to connect the Mediterranean Sea with the Red Sea, making it a vital link between Europe

and India and the Far East. The following year, he arranged for **Queen Victoria (1819-1901)** to be crowned **Empress of India,** a country that had been under varying degrees of British control for over a century and was now seen as the "crown jewel" of the British Empire. Disraeli also played a key role in redrawing boundaries of the Balkan countries of southeastern Europe following the **Russo-Turkish War (1877-1878),** effectively loosening Russia's de facto control of Turkey.

Though Disraeli did not serve in the capacity of prime minister as long as his rival, **William Ewart Gladstone** (see page 72), he is remembered as Queen Victoria's "favorite" prime minister due to the key role he played in the advancement of the British Empire during the century when it attained its greatest grandeur.

Benjamin Disraeli.

Italian revolutionary **Giuseppe Garibaldi** was the man whose leadership provided the catalyst that led to the unification of Italy for the first time since the time of the Roman emperors. Born in Nice, in present-day France, he joined the nationalist movement led by the Genovese patriot **Giuseppe Mazzini (1805-1872)** when he was in his twenties.

After the fall of the **Roman Empire** in the fifth century, Italy disintegrated into a mass of independent city-states. During the late **Middle Ages,** several city-states, such as Venice and Genoa, became world-class trading powers, and during the **Renaissance,** Florence, the capital of Tuscany, became the hub of art and culture. By the eighteenth century, however, the power of the great city-states had waned and outside powers, such as Spain, France and especially Austria, came to dominate Italy politically. In 1796, **Napoleon Bonaparte** (see page 62) swept into Italy and weakened Austrian control in much of northern Italy. He then incorporated Nice and Savoy into France—where they remain today—and much of the rest of the country, including Tuscany. Elsewhere in Italy, he redesigned city-states as republics on the French model.

By the 1830s, many groups, such as Mazzini's **Young Italian Society,** had begun to call for the establishment of a unified and independent Italy. Garibaldi, then a soldier of fortune and guerrilla leader, was typical of the young men who rallied to the cause of Italian freedom. Forced to flee the country in 1834, he spent time in the United States and then fought in the **Rio Grande Rebellion** in Brazil in 1836. In 1848, when revolution erupted in France and Austria and the people of Italy also rose up in rebellion, he returned home to join the patriots operating in and around Rome. Forced to flee a sec-

Giuseppe Garibaldi.

ond time, he went to the United States but in 1859 he returned to Italy.

On May 11, 1860, Garibaldi landed on the island of Sicily with 1000 men—known as "The Thousand" or the "red shirts" because of the distinctive colored shirts they wore—to launch his military campaign. After conquering Sicily and setting up a provisional government, he joined forces with King **Victor Emmanuel II (1820-1878)** of Sardinia, who had annexed Lombardy into his kingdom in 1859. Together, they liberated the Italian states one by one. In 1861, Victor Emmanuel was crowned king of a unified Italy.

In 1866, Italy allied itself with Prussia in its war against Austria, and as a result Venice was assimilated by Italy later that same year. The Papal States were also incorporated but Rome continued to be protected by the French, which wanted the pope to remain independent from the kingdom of Italy. After the defeat of France by Prussia in the **Franco-Prussian War (1870-1871)** and the collapse of the French empire, Rome was annexed to Italy and became the capital of a completely unified Italy. Garibaldi went on to serve in Italian Parliament in 1874. He died on June 2 1882 at his home on the island of Caprera.

62. CHARLES DARWIN
1809-1882

Born in Shrewsbury, England, the grandson of the renowned pottery manufacturer **Josiah Wedgewood (1730-1795)**, **Charles Darwin** was educated at Cambridge, where he took an interest in science in general and the evolution of the natural world in particular. Until the early nineteenth century, it was generally believed that the Earth and our natural environment had been created literally as the Bible states and had remained more or less the same ever since. However, by Darwin's time, many scientists had come to believe that living things change over time as part of an evolutionary process. People who subscribe to this theory are known as **evolutionists.** People who believe the Bible to be the literal truth are known as **creationists.**

Creationists believe that all species—from oysters to humans—were created in the exact same form as we know them today and that they have always had the same form. Evolutionists believe that a species is capable of changing from generation to generation and that two similar yet distinct species—such as lions and tigers, for instance—may have had a common ancestor millions of years ago. While the idea of evolution had been discussed in Greece as early as the fifth century BC, Darwin was the first person to formulate a detailed theory.

Immediately after graduating from Cambridge, Darwin accepted a position as an unpaid naturalist on a five-year survey expedition aboard the vessel HMS *Beagle.* The *Beagle* left England in December 1831 and returned in October 1836. During its five-year voyage, the ship's crew surveyed South America, Australia, New Zealand and countless islands en route, and the energetic Darwin began to synthesize his theory of evolution. He discovered that on remote islands such as the Galapagos, species were remarkably different than re-

Charles Darwin.

lated species on the mainland. This led him to the conclusion that while they did have common ancestors, over the course of time, the dissimilar environments of the species had caused them to *evolve* differently.

Darwin continued to refine his theory of **natural selection,** which stated that species evolved because nature "selected" those plants and animals best suited to specific environments. It took him over 20 years to completely detail his theory, but when his book *The Origin of Species* finally appeared in 1859, it radically impacted the course and theory of biological science by changing peoples' perspective of world history and the environment in which they lived.

In 1871, Darwin published *The Descent of Man,* in which he speculated on the evolution of human beings, expressing the controversial theory that people had evolved from a non-human ancestor which they had in common with apes. He also wrote extensive scientific treatises on plant biology and such diverse topics as coral reefs, volcanic islands and the geology of South America.

63. ABRAHAM LINCOLN
1809-1865

Along with **George Washington** (see page 58), **Abraham Lincoln** is regarded as one of the most outstanding American presidents in history. Born in a log cabin near Hodgenville, Kentucky, on February 12, 1809, at the age of 19 helped to crew a flatboat that carried farm produce down the Ohio and Mississippi Rivers to New Orleans. In 1830, along with his father, step-mother and step-siblings, Lincoln moved to Decatur, Illinois, where he worked for a time splitting rails for fencing. In 1831, he left home and worked in a variety of jobs ranging from flatboat hand to storekeeper.

In 1834, Lincoln was elected to the Illinois State Legislature, serving until 1843. He became a lawyer in 1837 and was elected to the US House of Representatives in 1846, where he served one term before returning to Springfield, Illinois to practice law. An ardent **abolitionist** and outspoken critic of **slavery,** Lincoln engaged in a series of debates with noted orator and US Senator **Stephen Douglas (1813-1861)** about whether slavery should be legalized in new territories that became states. Douglas' **Kansas-Nebraska Act** would have repealed the **Missouri Compromise** that limited slavery to only those states where it had existed in 1820.

His brilliant oratory in the **Lincoln-Douglas Debates** made Lincoln nationally prominent, and the newly formed **Republican Party** chose him to run against Douglas for the US Senate seat in 1858. Although he lost, in 1860 the Republicans nominated him as a compromise candidate for the office of president. Meanwhile, the **Democratic Party** had split and produced two candidates, Douglas and **John Breckinridge,** a development that assured Lincoln's victory.

On February 4, 1861, shortly after Lincoln assumed office, the 11 southern states of Alabama, Arkansas, Florida, Georgia,

Abraham Lincoln.

Louisiana, North Carolina, Mississippi South Carolina, Texas and Virginia seced ed from the Union and formed the **Confed erate States of America** over the issues o states rights and slavery. Lincoln vowed t go to war to restore the Union, however, i was the Confederacy that initiated the firs battle when it attacked the US Army pos at Fort Sumter on April 12, 1861, ignitin the American **Civil War (1861-1865),** war of national preservation, between tw profoundly different views. The Nort wanted the United States to remain one na tion; the South wanted it to become tw separate nations. In a historic civil right move, on January 1, 1863, Lincoln pro mulgated the **Emancipation Proclama**

tion abolishing slavery, and through his advocacy, two years later on January 31, 1865 it became an amendment to the United States Constitution.

Despite the military and industrial superiority of the Union, the first major battle at **Bull Run** on July 21, 1861 was an overwhelming Confederate victory. Over the next two years, the Union forces attempted to go on the offensive, but Confederate General **Robert Edward Lee (1807-1870)** consistently outmaneuvered them. Lee constantly threatened to capture Washington, DC, while the Union troops could never even get within striking distance of Richmond, the Confederate capital.

The tide turned in July 1863 in what are remembered as two of the conflict's bloodiest confrontations. Lee's forces, attempting to invade the North, were stopped at **Gettysburg, Pennsylvania**, and Union General **Ulysses Simpson Grant (1822-1885)** captured the Confederate stronghold at **Vicksburg, Mississippi** on the Mississippi River. It was at the dedication of the military cemetery at Gettysburg that Lincoln delivered the **Gettysburg Address,** the greatest speech in American history. Lincoln vowed "that this nation, under God, shall have a new birth of freedom; and that government of the people, by the people, for the people, shall not perish from the Earth."

Abraham Lincoln's dream of a united country was at last secured. Unfortunately, Lincoln himself did not live to enjoy the fruits of his hard-won peace. On April 15, 1865, while watching a performance at Ford's Theater in Washington, DC, he was assassinated by unemployed actor and Confederate sympathizer **John Wilkes Booth (1838-1865).**

Lincoln began his career as a lawyer in 1837.

Born in Liverpool and educated at Christ Church, Oxford, **William Ewart Gladstone** served as prime minister of Great Britain four times (1868-1874, 1880-1885, 1886 and 1892-1894) and became one of the most dominant political figures of the Victorian era. He entered politics as a Conservative but made his enduring mark as a Liberal (**Whig**) and reformer. This change in politics was directly opposite that of his longtime rival **Benjamin Disraeli** (see page 67), who initially was a Liberal but later became a leading Conservative.

Gladstone was elected to Parliament from Newark in 1833 and was immediately recognized as a gifted speaker. He became vice-president of the Board of Trade in 1841 and served as colonial secretary in 1846. In 1852, he succeeded Disraeli as chancellor of the Exchequer (equivalent to the American secretary of the treasury) and held this post for three years, during which time he brought about many needed financial reforms.

Gladstone left Parliament to write a classical study, *Homer and the Homeric Age*, published in 1859, but he returned to government the following year as a member of the newly formed Liberal Party. In 1867, he became his party's leader and the following year he became prime minister, a position he held until 1874. During this time, which was his greatest ministry, Britain enjoyed economic prosperity both at home and abroad. He passed the **Irish Land Act** to give Irish tenant farmers security and discontinued the practice that made the Church of England the official church of predominantly Roman Catholic Ireland. He also implemented a public school system to guarantee an education to all children, abolished the selling of army commissions, and ended the practice of appointing civil servants by placing jobs on a competition basis.

William Ewart Gladstone.

Gladstone called for elections in 1874, lost to Disraeli and retired to pursue writing and research projects. He returned to Parliament in 1876 and led the opposition until 1880, when he formed his second government as prime minister. He served until 1885, was briefly supplanted by the Conservatives and returned to office in 1886. During his third government, Gladstone proposed **Irish Home Rule,** which would have established an Irish Parliament. Although his proposal was defeated, it was ultimately enacted in 1914, eight years before Ireland became independent. This controversial issue ended his government, but he returned in 1892 as an 83-year-old elder statesman to form a fourth government. A victim of failing health, he retired in 1894.

Gladstone served a total of 14 years as prime minister of Great Britain, longer than any of his contemporaries. Recalled today as a riveting speaker with a truly brilliant intellect, his political foresight and reform ideas rank him as perhaps the most outstanding statesman in British Parliamentary history.

65. CHARLES DICKENS
1812-1870

Considered by many to be the greatest English fiction writer of the nineteenth century and one of the most brilliant since **William Shakespeare** (see page 50), **Charles John Huffam Dickens** was born in Portsmouth, the son of a Navy clerk, and grew up in London. He was an avid reader, but was forced by his father's imprisonment for debt to give up school and go to work in a factory when he was 12. Even at this early age, he began to develop his enormous powers of perception that would ultimately make his writings so rich with memorable characters.

Dickens eventually worked at a series of jobs as a reporter for such newspapers as the *Truesun,* the *Mirror of Parliament* and the *Morning Chronicle,* where he honed his skill as a writer. By the early 1830s, he was creating amusing sketches of street scenes and daily life for the *Old Monthly Magazine.* In 1837, these were assembled into a single volume as *The Pickwick Papers.* His next two books, *Oliver Twist* (1838) and *Nicholas Nickleby* (1839) were melodramatic and sometimes humorous chronicles of the lives of two young men that were exceedingly complex in their purpose and focused on character development.

After attaining success with these early works, Dickens edited two weekly magazines, *Household Words* (1850-1859) and *All Year Round* (1859-1870) for which he wrote serialized dramas that eventually became books. In 1843, he published *A Christmas Carol,* probably his most famous work and one of the most influential books in the English language. Who can ever forget the plight of the crippled Tiny Tim and the anguish and enlightenment experienced by Ebenezar Scrooge?

Still, some of Dickens's greatest work was yet to come. His next masterpiece, and his greatest novel, *David Copperfield,* ap-

peared in 1849, a compelling and witty book in which the world Dickens creates is more vivid than it is real, yet the story seems completely believable. His greatest historical novel, *A Tale of Two Cities,* which centered on events in London and Paris during the French Revolution, was published in 1859. *Great Expectations* (1861) exuded his unparalleled genius for characterization and turns of phrase.

In his time, Dickens was extremely popular with the public, who eagerly awaited new installments of his serialized works each week. The more attention he got, the more he craved it. In 1867-1868, he made his second tour of the United States, making appearances and conducting readings on a hectic schedule. He returned to England exhausted and plunged directly into his mystery novel, *Edwin Drood,* but died suddenly at the age of 58 before he could finish it. Since his death, Dickens's reputation as one of the most accomplished writers in the English language has continued to grow, and today many of his works are considered true classics.

Charles Dickens.

Born at Schönhausen in the Prussian (now German) state of Saxony, **Otto Eduard Leopold von Bismarck** was the son of a retired cavalry captain and grew up in a military environment. After studying law at the Universities of Greifswald and Göttingen, he represented his district in the Diet of Prussian Provinces from 1847. He opposed the leftist revolution of 1848 and, like many of his countrymen, believed it desirable for the German-speaking states to become unified as a single nation.

By the time Napoleon was defeated at Waterloo in 1815, the more than 300 German states that existed in the Middle Ages had combined into 39. Among these states were powerful nations, such as Austria and Prussia, and other, smaller states, such as Bavaria and Saxony. However, efforts to unify Germany after the Napoleonic era always resulted in a competition between Prussia and Austria over which would be the dominant entity in a united Germany. Ultimately, Prussia emerged as the most powerful of the German states, and Austria has remained separate from the unified Germany ever since, except for the period from 1938 to 1945.

Bismarck was to become the man most responsible for charting the course of German unification. In 1851, he was appointed as the Prussian envoy to the Bundestag (the diet or council of Germans states) by King **Friedrich Wilhelm IV (1795-1861).** He later served as the Prussian ambassador to France, where he was amused by the corruption within the French court. This experience provided him with valuable insights that would later serve him well. In 1862, Friedrich Wilhelm's brother and heir, **Wilhelm I (1797-1888),** named Bismarck chancellor of Prussia. Known as the "Iron Chancellor," Bismarck went on to serve as the first chancellor of the German Empire from 1871 to 1890.

Bismarck.

By 1866, Austria was defeated (but not annexed) and Bismarck had engineered a unification of most of the German states under Prussian control, and he needed only to demonstrate Prussia's military power in order to guarantee supremacy over all of Germany. Meanwhile, **Louis Napoleon (1808-1873)** (Emperor **Napoleon III** after 1852) had announced his intentions of extending France's eastern border to the Rhine River and incorporating many German states into the French Empire. On July 19, 1870, Napoleon declared war on the German states, igniting the **Franco-Prussian War (1870-1871).** Thanks to shrewd planning by Bismarck, Prussia was well prepared for such an attack. The Germans counterattacked, reaching Paris by Christmas Day.

After winning a decisive victory, Prussia possessed the political power to unite the Germans. On January 18, 1871, the German Empire, or **Reich,** was established, with Bismarck as its chancellor. Bismarck then undertook judiciary, monetary and administrative reforms to integrate the German states. He also engineered a complex network of international treaties designed to isolate France, which he viewed as Germany's primary enemy in Europe.

Bismarck continued to be the power behind the throne until 1890 when **Wilhelm II (1859-1941)** asked him to resign. Feeling bitter, Bismarck retired to his castle near Hamburg to write his memoirs in which he predicted **World War I (1914-1918)** and Germany's defeat.

67. JULES VERNE
1829-1905

French author **Jules Verne** was a visionary genius who invented the genre of **science fiction,** predicting scientific developments and human adventures that were practically beyond the imagination of his time. Railroads and steam locomotives were not yet a reality when he was born, yet he wrote detailed accounts of long distance air travel, ocean-going submarines and how one day humans would fly to the Moon! The technology to make all of these things possible did ultimately evolve, but during Verne's lifetime, they were still just fantastic possibilities.

Born the son of a lawyer in Nantes, Verne grew up dreaming of world travel. Although he was sent to Paris to study law, he instead took up writing fiction stories for magazines. His first book, *Five Weeks in a Balloon* (1863), was a best-seller. His success continued with *A Journey to the Center of the Earth* in 1864 and *Twenty Thousand Leagues Under the Sea* in 1870, the latter of which featured the legendary arch-villain **Captain Nemo,** skipper of the enormous submarine, *Nautilus*. In 1865, he published part one of *From the Earth to the Moon, and A Trip Around It*. Part two appeared in serial form in the late 1860s and as a book in 1870.

Riding the crest of public interest in science and invention in the nineteenth century, Verne's books became immensely popular. Not only were they well-paced adventure stories, but they also transported readers to places they had never been before. Not only did Verne focus the action of his novels in yet unexplored locations like outer space, the bottom of the ocean and deep inside the Earth, but in novels such as *The Children of Captain Grant* (1868), he carried his readers to South America and Australia, lands that were just as remote and exotic for most European readers as the Moon.

Jules Verne.

Readers also loved Verne's books because they had thrilling, fast-paced plots. In the immortal classic *Around the World in Eighty Days* (1873), the engaging hero **Phineas Fogg** is constantly in motion, never pausing for more than a couple of days in any one place, because he is taking part in the race of his lifetime.

Verne was as hard-working and prolific a writer as he was successful. Between 1878 and 1880 he published four novels as well as a three-volume history of exploration entitled *The Discovery of the Earth*. In his later years, he indulged his continuing passion for invention with *Clipper of the Clouds* (1886) in which he imagined fleets of gargantuan airships populating the sky—an idea that not only accurately foreshadowed the era of the *Hindenberg* and other airships of the 1930s but the jumbo jets that appeared in the 1970s.

Verne studied science and geography to give his science fiction a basis in fact. He also strived for clarity so even young readers could enjoy his books and "so as not to suffer even a line to escape from my pen which the boys, for whom I write and whom I love, cannot read."

68. CHIEF SITTING BUFFALO BULL (TATANKYA IYOTAKE) 1834-1890

In the Western Hemisphere, Europeans and their descendants engaged in open conflict with the native peoples of the Americas from 1492 until the dawn of the twentieth century. In the United States, official government policy toward the Indians alternated between ignoring them and consciously removing them from specific areas. In the vast plains and prairies of the West, which attracted few pioneers, the nomadic native peoples generally managed to avoid settlers until the years after the American **Civil War (1861-1865)**. Even then, encounters between the two groups were only sporadic, taking place primarily along emigrant trails.

However, between 1866 and 1868, a series of battles fought in the North Plains brought about the final end to the native way of life. In this period there were a number of leaders among the Plains Indians who came to the forefront. **Red Cloud (1822-1909)** of the Oglala Sioux led his people in the so-called **Red Cloud's War (1866-1868)** and concluded the **Fort Laramie Treaty** that remained in force for eight years before it was broken by gold seekers staking claims in the Dakota Territory that the treaty had permanently promised to the Sioux. The messianic and enigmatic Oglala Sioux Chief Shaman **Crazy Horse (Tashuncahuitco) (1849-1877)** resisted confinement to a reservation and led the Sioux uprising of 1875-1877. Chief **Joseph (Hinmaton-Yalatkit) (1830-1904)** of the Nez Perce won an incredible series of battles against the US Army before surrendering in 1877 with words that proved to be an epitaph for the Plains warriors: "From where the Sun now stands, I will fight no more, forever."

However, there was no leader who more fully embodied the courage and tenacity of the Native Americans' final stand against the inevitable westward movement of white settlers than Hunkpapa Sioux chief **Sitting Buffalo Bull,** generally known as **Sitting Bull.** Born in present-day South Dakota, he became a respected warrior and later a war chief. Rejecting the Fort Laramie Treaty, he and Crazy Horse and their followers refused to relocate to Dakota Territory.

In 1876, when the American government broke the treaty, the Sioux and their Cheyenne allies returned to Montana where Sitting Bull formed the nucleus of a great **Gathering of Tribes.** To force the Indians to return to the reservation, several US Army units, including those led by General **George Cook (1829-1890)** and the flamboyant Colonel **George Armstrong Custer (1839-1876),** staged a three-pronged attack. Custer, anxious for glory, was the first to make contact with the Sioux. What he had not been able to foresee, however, was that Indian leaders had assembled the largest encampment of warriors ever encountered by the US Army. Over 3000 Sioux and Cheyenne, under the leadership of Sitting Bull, had gathered on the banks of the Little Bighorn River. Foolishly, Custer attacked, and he and his 215-man force were wiped out in 45 minutes. **The Battle of the Little Bighorn** on June 25, 1876 was the biggest Indian victory in all the North American Indian wars.

Although the Indians won this battle, they inevitably lost the war. The US Army launched a major offensive to punish the Sioux for the fiasco at Little Bighorn, but Sitting Bull managed to escape to Canada, where he remained until 1881. He returned to the United States a folk hero, going on to appear in **Buffalo Bill's Wild West Show** in 1886. In 1890, when the **Ghost Dance** movement inspired the Plains tribes with visions of a utopian future without white men, Sitting Bull was implicated, and he was shot and killed by Indian police while "resisting arrest" in Dakota Territory.

Writer and humorist **Samuel Clemens,** one of the most influential and well-loved writers in American literary history, was born in Florida, Missouri. His most famous works include *Life on the Mississippi* (1883), *The Adventures of Tom Sawyer* (1876) and *The Adventures of Huckleberry Finn* (1884), which were based on his experiences growing up in Hannibal, Missouri, a town on the Mississippi River, where he met people from all walks of life who traveled by steamboat, including show folk, gamblers, preachers and con men.

After his father died when he was 12, Clemens went to work as an apprentice typesetter, which allowed him the opportunity to read a variety of books. In 1852, he began writing humorous stories for the *Hannibal Journal.* After working as a typesetter in various towns from St. Louis to Cincinnati, Ohio, to New York City, he worked for a time as a river boat pilot. The phrase **"Mark Twain,"** which he later adopted as his pen name, is taken from a code used by Mississippi river men meaning "two fathoms down," indicating a particular river channel depth.

Clemens once worked as a river boat pilot.

When the **Civil War (1861-1865)** began, Clemens served briefly in the Confederate Army before heading West to the silver and gold mining areas of Nevada and California. Between 1864 and 1867, he worked for several newspapers in San Francisco. Published in 1867, his first book, *The Celebrated Jumping Frog of Calaveras County,* was a collection of short stories celebrating life on the western frontier. That same year, he traveled in Europe and the Middle East and he later satirically recounted his observations in the book *Innocents Abroad* (1869).

In 1869, he settled in Buffalo, New York, as part owner of a newspaper and married **Olivia Langdon** in 1870. He continued to write newspaper columns and the amazing tales of Tom and Huck. He also wrote *The Prince and the Pauper* (1882) and *A Connecticut Yankee in King Arthur's Court* (1889), historical novels laced with his characteristic wit and humor.

In his lifetime, Clemens's books were quite successful, but he unwisely invested his earnings and in 1894, Charles L. Webster & Company, the firm in which he was a part owner, went bankrupt. This, and the deaths of his daughter **Susan** in 1895 and his wife in 1904 deeply depressed him. He published *Personal Recollections of Joan of Arc* in 1896 and *Following the Equator* in 1897, which earned him enough money to pay off his debts. His last work, *The Mysterious Stranger,* was finished in 1898 but published posthumously in 1916.

Thomas Alva Edison.

When one makes a list of history's greatest inventors, one name always percolates to the top. **Thomas Alva Edison,** once known as "the wizard," invented not one but three major devices which became essential parts of the fabric of daily life: the **phonograph,** the **electric light bulb** and **motion pictures.**

Born in Milan, Ohio, on February 11, 1847, Edison was educated primarily at home by his mother, **Nancy Elliot Edison,** a high school teacher. In 1863, he became a telegrapher, first on the Grand Trunk Railroad and later for several other companies. Although he invented several devices for improving telegraphy, his first patents in 1869 were for the **electrographic vote recorder** and the **stock ticker.** After selling the latter patent for an incredible $40,000, he used the money to equip a laboratory in Menlo Park, New Jersey.

The phonograph was one of Edison's first projects. In August 1877, he displayed a cylinder wrapped in a thin sheet of foil and on December 6, he made a recording of himself reciting *Mary Had a Little Lamb* that still survives today. His first phonograph, which he called a "talking machine," was powered by a hand crank, but the sound tempo was so inconsistent that in 1878 he built one with an electric motor. He developed an improved phonograph model in 1886 in partnership with **Charles Sumner Tainter (1854-1940)** and **Chichester Bell,** a cousin of **Alexander Graham Bell** (see page 80), the inventor of the telephone as well as wax records for Edison's phonograph.

The electric light bulb was actually invented in 1879 simultaneously by Edison in the United States and **Sir Joseph Wilson Swan (1828-1914)** in England. The problem to be solved was devising the right conductor, or filament, and inserting it in a container, or bulb, without oxygen because the presence of oxygen caused filament to burn. Although Swan was the first to construct an electric light bulb, he had trouble maintaining a vacuum in his bulb. Edison overcame this dilemma, and on October 21, 1879, he illuminated a carbon filament light bulb that continued to glow for 40 hours. By the end of 1880, he had produced a 16-watt bulb that could last for 1500 hours and began marketing his new invention.

The invention of motion pictures was a much more complex process, involving numerous other inventions such as photography and eventually sound recording. However, the key idea behind motion pictures came with the discovery that when a series of closely spaced, sequential still pictures—such as that of a child skipping rope or a horse running—are viewed in rapid succession, the viewer experiences an illusion of movement. This phenomenon known as the **persistence of vision,** was first understood by **Leonardo da Vinci** (see page 42).

In the nineteenth century, inventors produced various hand-held devices in which images arranged on a spinning wheel or disk appeared to move. However, what all of these mechanisms had in common was that they used images printed on an opaque surface for direct viewing. The next evolutionary step that led to motion pictures occurred in 1889 when Edison in the United States and **William Friese-Greene (1855-1921)** in England each decided to print multiple images on a transparent material that could be projected. Edison adapted his method for use in his **kinetograph,** which was the first camera specifically designed to film motion pictures and his **kinetoscope,** which was the first motion picture projector. Both were patented in 1891, and the kinetoscope debuted in New York as a peep-show device in 1893. Because he failed to patent these inventions abroad, it was possible for two brothers in France named **Auguste (1862-1954)** and **Louis (1864-1948) Lumière** to build what amounted to an improved version of his kinetograph, which they called **cinematographie.** Although Edison had built a movie studio in New Jersey in 1893, his former associate **William Dickson** founded American Biograph, the first motion picture production company.

Edison's electric light bulb.

In 1887, Edison opened his **Invention Factory** in West Orange, New Jersey, where he employed a staff of 1200 that turned out dozens of important inventions, including the **automatic telegraph** and the **storage battery.**

Edison's phonograph.

79

The inventor of the **telephone, Alexander Graham Bell,** was born in Edinburgh, Scotland, the son of **Alexander Melville Bell (1819-1905),** the inventor of a physiological alphabet for deaf people that gave the eye a guide to the making of oral sound. He studied at universities in Edinburgh and London before emigrating to the United States in 1871 to demonstrate his father's alphabet.

In 1873, Bell became a professor of vocal physiology at Boston University, where he began experimenting with acoustics and developed the concept of transmitting speech electrically. Ultimately, this led to the invention of the telephone. According to the famous story, the first fully intelligible telephone call occurred on March 6, 1876, when Bell, in one room, called to his assistant, **Thomas Watson,** in another room: "Come here, Watson, I want you." Watson heard the request through a receiver connected to the transmitter that Bell had designed.

Although **Elisha Gray (1835-1901)** had built the first steel diaphragm/electromagnet receiver in 1874, he was not able to master the design of a workable transmitter until after Bell did. Bell had worked tirelessly, experimenting with various types of mechanisms, while Gray became discouraged. Incredibly, both men filed for a patent on their designs at the New York patent office on February 14, 1876, with

Alexander Graham Bell.

Bell beating Gray by only two hours! Gra later challenged Bell's patent but the U Supreme Court ruled in Bell's favor.

In 1877, Bell founded the **Bell Tele phone Company,** which later grew in **American Telephone & Telegrap (AT&T),** the largest telephone company the world. Bell Telephone opened the fir transcontinental telephone line from Ne York to San Francisco in 1915. Bell, wl went on to enjoy great financial success, well as public acclaim, for the telephon also invented tl **photophone** and tl **audiometer,** as we as flat and cylind cal **wax phon graph records.** B retired but remain active as a regent the **Smithsonian I stitution** in Was ington, DC.

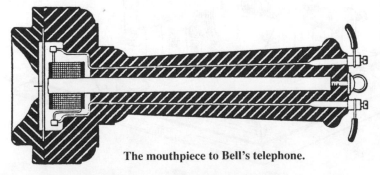

The mouthpiece to Bell's telephone.

Mutsuhito, (Moo-tsoo-hē′tō), also known as **Meiji,** the man who initiated the reforms that ultimately made Japan a modern nation and a world power, became the 122nd emperor of his country in 1867 when he was 15 years old. While the emperor was considered the absolute figurehead ruler, or **tenshi** ("son of heaven"), Japan had in fact been ruled for 700 years by a hereditary class of feudal lords known as **shoguns.**

In the mid-nineteenth century, Japan was still a feudal monarchy. Being an island nation, it was geographically isolated from mainland Asia—and indeed from the rest of the world—completely removed from the mainstream of world history, which was exactly how the emperors and shoguns preferred it. On July 8, 1853, US Navy Commodore **Matthew Calbraith Perry 1794-1858)** sailed into Edo Bay with a squadron of heavily armed gunboats and a message from President **Millard Fillmore 1800-1874):** Japan should open its harbors to American trade or risk war.

Perry gave Japan the better part of a year to consider this ultimatum, and when he returned, the **Treaty of Kanawa** (Kə-nä′-wə) was signed on March 31, 1854. Japan had finally joined the world community. By 1858, the United States, Britain and France had established supply bases in Japan but there was a good deal of unrest. Mutsuhito expressly prohibited anti-foreign activities and initiated a program to modernize Japan by importing machines and machine tools from the leading edge of the Industrial Revolution. At the time of Perry's first landing at Edo Bay in 1853, Japan was the technological equivalent of Europe in the 1550s.

Within a quarter century of the **Meiji Reformation** of 1868, Japan had industrialized to the technological level of Europe and the United States. It was an effort that the world had never before witnessed, with the possible exception of Japan's resurrection after the devastation of **World War II (1939-1945).** Japan entered the twentieth century as the leading power in Asia.

Mutsuhito recognized the value of international trade that had been so vitally important to Japan's success in the world. He moved Japan's seat of government from remote Kyoto to the commercially strategic city of Kyoto and took an active role in guiding Japan through what came to be known as the **Era of Enlightenment.**

Japanese warriors of the mid-nineteenth century.

Sigmund Freud.

The originator of the practice of **psychoanalysis** and the first person to complete a major clinical study of the human **subconscious, Sigmund Freud** was born in Freiburg, Moravia, but spent almost all his life in Vienna. Educated at the University of Vienna, he received his M.D. in 1881. He helped discover the anesthetic properties of cocaine, and in 1886 he studied briefly under French neuropsychiatrist **Jean Martin Charcot (1825-1893).** In 1886, he set up his medical practice in Vienna as a specialist in nervous disease. His first published work, *Aphasia* (1891), was a study of this neurological disorder.

Freud became interested in the subconscious and, in collaboration with **Josef Breuer,** wrote a series of papers on the subject of **hysteria** that were published in 1895. It was at this time that he developed the theory that mental illness and personality disturbances were rooted in unpleasant sexual experiences during childhood. He theorized that the mind functions on three levels: the **conscious,** the **unconscious** and the **preconscious.** He also believed that people repress feelings and memories from the preconscious or conscious to the unconscious and that lengthy conversations with a **psychotherapist,** known as **psychotherapy,** could help uncover, and relieve the pain of, these repressed feelings and memories.

In 1900, Freud published *The Interpretation of Dreams,* in which he sought to quantify and categorize the complex activities of the human subconscious. In 1906, he co-founded the **International Congress of Psychoanalysis** with several colleagues, including **Alfred Adler (1870-1937)** and **Carl Gustav Jung (1875-1961).** Freud's obsession with sex as the overwhelming motivation in human activity eventually prompted Alder and Jung to go their separate ways. Adler focused his work on **Individual Psychology,** theorizing that there were numerous factors, not just sex, that formed a person's conscious and subconscious and that these varied from one individual to another. Jung turned his energies to the study of the importance of mythology, cultural symbolism and individual creativity and how they helped to shape personality. Among his most important work are *The Integration of the Personality* (1939), *Memories and Reflections* and *Man and His Symbols.*

In 1938, when **Adolf Hitler** (see page 97) incorporated Austria into Germany, Freud emigrated to London, where he died of cancer the following year. After his death, the popularity of psychoanalysis, the medical discipline which he founded, continued to grow, especially in the United States in the two decades following World War II. Today, the therapeutic approaches he pioneered continue to be used in modified forms by many psychiatrists to treat various mental disorders, such as **psychoses** and **neuroses.**

Theodore Roosevelt, the American president who defined the role of the United States as a superpower in the early twentieth century, was born in New York City on October 17, 1858. A sickly child, he later sought to overcome his early handicaps by adopting the lifestyle of a rugged outdoorsman. In 1880, he graduated from Harvard University and married **Alice Hathaway Lee.** After she died in 1884, he took their daughter **Alice** (who later married Congressman Nicholas Longworth in a White House ceremony) to live on a ranch in North Dakota. During his years there, he wrote several books on the American West. In 1886, he married **Edith Kermit Carow** and they had five children.

In 1889, Roosevelt was appointed to the US Civil Service Commission, where he became a reformer, fighting the **spoils system** of rewarding political influence rather than merit in government employment. In 1897, he was appointed secretary of the Navy under President **William McKinley 1843-1901)** and directed the modernization of the US Navy fleet. The following year, the USS *Maine* was blown up while anchored in the harbor at Havana, Cuba, and the **Spanish-American War (1898)** began. Roosevelt immediately resigned from his government post to organize the **First Volunteer Cavalry** (the **"Rough Riders"**), a US Army regiment composed primarily of cowboys and lawmen from the American West. The regiment distinguished itself in Cuba and Roosevelt personally led the now-famous charge against Spanish forces on **San Juan Hill.**

After the war ended later that year, Roosevelt was elected governor of the state of New York. In 1900, the Republican Party nominated him to run as the vice-presidential candidate to William McKinley. They won the election, and when McKinley was assassinated on September 14, 1901, Roosevelt became the youngest man (at age 42) to ever serve as president of the United States. He was elected by a landslide in 1904 but chose not to stand for re-election in 1908.

As president, Roosevelt had numerous accomplishments. He established the **Interstate Commerce Commission (ICC)** to regulate the railroads, he supported the passage of the **Pure Food & Drug Act,** personally resolved the 1902 coal strike and expanded America's public land reserves. He was the catalyst for launching construction on the historic **Panama Canal** to link the Atlantic and Pacific oceans, and he helped mediate the end of the **Russo-Japanese War (1904-1905).** He created the US Navy's **Great White Fleet** and then sent it on an around-the-world tour to underscore America's role as a superpower.

After stepping down from the presidency, Roosevelt traveled widely in Europe, as well as in Africa, where he continued to perpetuate his image as a vigorous sportsman. In 1912, he again ran for president, this time as the candidate of the **Progressive (Bull Moose) Party.** Although he lost to Democrat **Woodrow Wilson (1856-1924),** he received more votes than the Republican Party candidate.

In 1913, Roosevelt wrote his official autobiography, although he had already published several books about his life. While traveling in South America, he led a scientific expedition to the upper Amazon River 1914 where he discovered the **River of Doubt.** He then retired to write further accounts of his adventures. During **World War I (1914-1918),** he considered organizing another volunteer regiment, but finally decided against it. He died at his home in Long Island, New York, on January 6, 1919, having lived as full a life as any man could ever expect.

Henry Ford.

Born near Dearborn, outside of Detroit, Michigan, **Henry Ford** took an early interest in the mechanical inner workings of the devices and machines that were invented during the **Industrial Revolution** and became commonplace in the United States by the latter nineteenth century. Trained as a machinist, he became chief engineer of the Edison Company in 1887.

The **internal combustion engine** was invented in Germany by **Nikolaus Otto (1852-1891)** when Ford was 13. The **automobile,** invented in Germany by **Gottlieb Daimler (1834-1900)** and **Wilhelm Maybach (1846-1929)**—powered by an internal combustion engine—arrived on the scene when he was 26. A novelty when first introduced, automobiles inspired people of Ford's generation who saw the vast potential in what their elders still considered a silly, impractical machine. Ford constructed his first automobile at his home in Detroit in 1893 and quit Edison four years later to devote himself full-time to their manufacture. With $28,000, he founded the **Ford Motor Company** in 1903 and introduced the Ford **Model A** that same year.

Prior to this time, automobiles were, for the most part, custom-made, one-of-a-kind machines. The first quantity-produced automobile was the 1901 **Curved Dash Oldsmobile** built by **Ransom E. Olds (1864-1950),** another Detroit mechanic, but his Oldsmobiles were made slowly, one at a time.

Ford conceived the idea of an **assembly line,** on which machines, materials and men were situated in the order that they entered into the assembly of an automobile. Mechanical means were used to deliver parts when, where and in the quantities that they were needed. To insure an even flow of work, each employee was assigned a few specialized tasks that required an equal amount of time to complete. Over the entire length of the line, all assembly operations were performed simultaneously and work in process was transmitted continuously, at a uniform rate, from one work station to the next. The assembly line not only made it possible to build vehicles many times faster than by any previous method, it also allowed the company to double workers' salaries and reduce the work day from nine to eight hours, while still offering a lower retail price to consumers.

It can truly be said that Ford put America on wheels. After he introduced his **Model T** in 1908, his assembly line produced 15 million over the next 19 years. In 1927, Ford introduced a new **Model A,** building five million by 1932. By 1942, when American automobile production was suspended in order for factories to produce war supplies, 30 million Fords had been sold.

Henry Ford served as president of the Ford Motor Company until 1919, when his son **Edsel Ford (1893-1943)** took over. After Edsel's death, Ford resumed control until after World War II, when he was succeeded by his grandson, **Henry Ford II.**

Wilbur Wright was born in Millville, Indiana, and his brother **Orville** was born in Dayton, Ohio, where they later opened a small bicycle manufacturing shop. Both took an active interest in **aeronautics** and in the dream held by many young men of their era: that of building a flying machine capable of carrying a person.

At the end of the eighteenth century, the Montgolfier brothers in France built the first lighter-than-air balloon that was capable of carrying people aloft. Still, the dream of human flight in a *controlled heavier-than-air* vehicle remained elusive. (Heavier-than-air implies a vehicle that is held aloft by its aerodynamic properties rather than by a bag of gas.) Several attempts at building such a machine were undertaken without success in the late nineteenth century. One failed attempt, by **Samuel Pierpont Langley (1834-1906)** and the **Smithsonian Institution,** was abandoned literally days before the Wrights' first successful flight.

The Wright Brothers had built their first unmanned glider in 1896, and between 1900 and 1902 they tested a series of manned gliders at Kill Devil Hill on North Carolina's windswept **Kitty Hawk Peninsula.** They recognized that the key to successful powered flight would be the degree of control which the pilot could exercise over his craft. They looked upon their project as an *aircraft* rather than as a modified kite or as a machine that would be controlled in the air as a boat was in the water. The first **Wright Flyer** was a fabric-covered biplane with a wooden frame driven by the Wrights' own 12hp water-cooled engine connected to two contra-rotating propellers by means of belts. Wilbur and Orville completed their Flyer during the summer of 1903 and took it to Kitty Hawk in December. On the 13th, Wilbur took the first turn and succeeded only in nosing the Flyer into a dune. On December 17, however, Orville took to the air for 12 seconds,

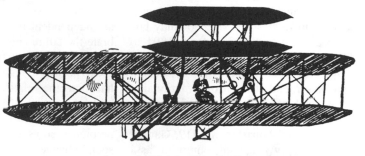

An early Wright Flyer in flight.

covering 120 feet (37 meters) in the first powered flight of a manned heavier-than-air craft in history. By the end of the day, each had made two successful flights, with Wilbur covering 852 feet (260 meters) in his last turn at the controls.

Starting on May 13, 1904, their **Flyer 2** made a number of successful flights over the next seven months. Like the original Flyer, however, it manifested a tendency to stall in turns, and the Wrights went back to the drawing board. The result was the larger **Flyer 3,** which proved to be a much more reliable airplane, and was able to fly successfully over a distance of 34 miles (55 km). On October 5, 1905, it set an endurance record of 38 minutes aloft.

The brothers made numerous demonstration flights in the United States and Europe and founded the **American Wright Company** in 1909. Wilbur died of typhoid fever in 1912 and Orville sold his interest in 1915 to devote himself to his work as director of the **Wright Aeronautical Laboratory** in Dayton.

The man who stands as the symbol of nonviolent resistance to political and social repression, **Mohandas Gandhi** was born on October 2, 1869, at Porbandar in British-dominated India, the son of the prime minister to the maharajah of the state of Porbandar. His mother, a member of the vegetarian **Jainist** religion, influenced him in his pursuit of nonviolence. He went to England in 1882 to study law and practiced in Bombay from 1891 to 1893 and in South Africa until 1914.

Upon his return to India in 1915, Gandhi became sympathetic with the nationalist movement aimed at ending British rule. After British troops massacred hundreds of nationalists at Amristar in 1919, Gandhi became deeply involved, emerging as a leader of the **Indian National Congress.** He traded a suit and tie for the simple clothes of the "untouchables," India's lowest social class. He preached simplicity and even insisted that his growing number of followers weave their own cloth, and soon the spinning wheel became the insignia of the Congress, even enduring to the present day as a central feature on the Indian flag.

Taking the name **Mahatma,** meaning "great soul," Gandhi found himself the spiritual leader of a movement that attracted thousands, and eventually millions, to the cause of Indian independence. Although he advocated nonviolence, he also promoted the idea of non-cooperation with British rulers, one notable example of which is his 1930 boycott in protest of the British tax on salt. As a result of the success of this and other protests and his unwavering support for a total British withdrawal from India, he was jailed several times by British authorities.

After World War II, the idea of the British leaving India, which would have been unthinkable even a decade earlier, had gained a great deal of momentum, and by 1947 the British flag was lowered for the last time. Most of British India, where **Hinduism** was the dominant religion, became the nation of **India,** while the areas where there was a **Moslem** majority became **Pakistan.** Gandhi strongly opposed the partitioning of India, but he was unable to prevent it.

Although Mahatma Gandhi lived to see an independent India, he was able to celebrate the culmination of his life's work for only a very short time. On January 30, 1948, he was assassinated by a Hindu who harbored the mistaken belief that Gandhi had become pro-Moslem. However, the use of nonviolent political protests, which he pioneered as a means of bringing about social change, continues to be a model for other great leaders to follow.

Mohandas Gandhi.

79. NIKOLAI LENIN (VLADIMIR ILYICH ULIANOV) 1870-1924

Nikolai Lenin.

Nikolai Lenin, the man who imposed **communism** on the crumbling **Russian Empire,** was born in Simbursk (later Ulyanovsk), Russia, the son of a minor nobleman and the younger brother of a revolutionary executed for plotting against the Russian emperor, Tsar **Alexander III (1845-1894).** In the 1890s, Lenin and others dedicated themselves to overthrowing the monarchy of the Russian Empire, the largest, fully contiguous nation in the world. Despite its size, Russia had remained a backward, primitive place, barely touched by the Industrial Revolution or the social improvements that impacted Europe during the previous century.

Ruled by the autocratic tsars of the **Romanov Dynasty,** Russia's inhabitants became increasingly restless. There had been an uprising in 1905 after Russia had lost the **Russo-Japanese War (1904-1905),** but Tsar **Nicholas II (1868-1918)** successfully suppressed it. In 1914, Russia went to war against the Germans in **World War I (1914-1918).** After Nicholas' armies suffered defeat on the battlefield, the domestic situation began to unravel. The entire social and economic structure of the Russian Empire finally collapsed under its own weight and the strain of the war. Numerous food riots occurred in 1915 and 1916, and in 1917, a full-scale revolution erupted. On March 2, 1917, the tsar was forced to abdicate.

Several failed attempts to establish a new government followed. As anarchy and starvation swept the countryside, Russia became fertile ground for the doctrine of socialism preached by German academic and philosopher **Karl Marx (1818-1883),** whose Communist theory held that the masses could have all they needed by simply seizing the property of the rich. The most violent and organized of the socialist groups were the **Bolsheviks,** who had ve-

hemently opposed the tsar. When the Constitutional Democrats, led by **Alexander Kerensky (1881-1970),** set up a government, they attacked him as well. On November 7, 1917, Kerensky was toppled in a bloody coup and the Bolsheviks seized power, establishing a Council of People's Commissars to govern Russia. Lenin, who had been living in Switzerland when the revolution broke out, became head of the Council and the first premier of post-Imperial Russia.

Lenin's new government encountered a great deal of opposition, but in March 1918, he signed a peace treaty with the Germans and was able to bring troops loyal to his cause home to silence those who disagreed with him. Lenin had the tsar and his family executed but retained his empire by simply renaming his colonies as "Soviet Socialist Republics" and incorporating them into a new Russian Empire in 1922 that he called the **Union of Soviet Socialist Republics (USSR).** Lenin died on January 21, 1924 in the village of Gorky outside of Moscow and was succeeded by **Josef Stalin** (see page 91).

As prime minister of Great Britain during **World War II (1939-1945), Sir Winston Leonard Spencer Churchill** personified the determination of the British people to resist German aggression. Born on November 30, 1874 at Blenheim Palace outside Woodstock, Churchill was the son of a direct descendent of the first duke of Marlborough and **Jennie Jerome,** an American. An avid student of history, he attended Harrow and the Royal Military College at Sandhurst. He served in the British army for six years, heroically distinguishing himself in 1899 during the **Boer War (1899-1902)** in South Africa.

Elected to Parliament in 1900, Churchill went on to serve in the cabinet and as first lord of the Admiralty in 1911, where he played an important role in planning the modernization of the British fleet, a vital factor in Britain's naval successes in **World War I (1914-1918).** During this war, he returned to uniform briefly and later served as Minister of Munitions under Prime Minister **David Lloyd George (1863-1945).**

When George's government was defeated in 1922, Churchill left government service only to return in 1924 as Chancellor of the Exchequer. While out of government during the 1930s, Churchill became outspoken in his insistence that Britain prepare for war with Nazi Germany. When **Adolf Hitler** (see page 97) touched off World War II with his invasion of Poland on September 1, 1939, Britain and France declared war and Prime Minister **Neville Chamberlain (1869-1940)** gave Churchill his former job at the Admiralty. In May 1940, after a succession of German victories and Allied failures, Chamberlain resigned and Churchill took his place as prime minister.

France surrendered on June 22, leaving Britain to face the onslaught of Germany's

Churchill.

blitzkrieg alone. While German forces prepared for a cross-channel invasion of Britain, the English people rallied around Churchill on May 10 after he told them he had "nothing to offer but blood, toil, tears and sweat." He defied Hitler by informing him that his troops would meet relentless opposition on the beaches, on the streets and in every village. In fact, pilots of the Royal Air Force (RAF), who met the Germans, were able to destroy 12 bombers for each one of their own losses. Churchill called it the RAF's "finest hour."

Indeed, it was Churchill's finest hour. He had met Hitler eyeball to eyeball, and Hitler had blinked. Germany called off its planned invasion of Britain. Although Hitler's forces would not be defeated for nearly five more years, Britain had survived, due in large part because her people had a tenacious leader who had truly inspired them. Churchill met with American President **Franklin Roosevelt** (see page 94) numerous times, both before and after the United States entered the war in 1941 forming what Churchill called the **Grand Alliance** that was ultimately victorious.

In 1945, Churchill's Conservative Party was turned out of office, but he returned as prime minister in 1951 and served until 1955. Shortly after being knighted in 1953 he suffered a stroke that affected the pace of his affairs for the rest of his life. He died on January 24, 1965, leaving his mark on history as well as numerous historical books. His four-volume *History of the English Speaking Peoples* (1958) and the six-volume *The Second World War* (1954) are considered classics.

Born near Bologna, Italy, electrical engineer **Gugilelmo Marconi,** who invented the first practical wireless communication system, attended the University of Bologna, where he conducted his first experiments using electromagnetic waves for communications.

Both the **telegraph** (1838) and the **telephone** (1875) were enormous leaps forward in the evolution of communication technology. A major limitation of the technology was that the people using them had to be linked by a wire. If the wire was broken, or if a wire could not be run, then

Gugilelmo Marconi.

communication was impossible. In 1887, German scientist **Heinrich Hertz (1857-1894)** discovered radio waves, but it was Marconi who first adapted them for use in communications. Marconi's milestone occurred in 1895 when he succeeded in transmitting a wireless electronic message over a distance of a mile and a half (2.4 km) near Bologna.

Three years later, Eugene Ducretet and Ernest Roger transmitted a wireless message across the city of Paris, and on March 28, 1899, Marconi sent the first international wireless message from Dover, England to Wimereux, France, a distance of 31 miles (50 km). On December 12, 1901, he successfully conducted the first intercontinental wireless transmission between Poldhu, England and a receiving station in Newfoundland, 2100 miles (3400 km) away. In 1903, Marconi established a transmission station, designated WCC, in South Wellfleet, Massachusetts. The dedication ceremonies included an exchange of greetings between American President **Theodore Roosevelt** (see page 83) and King **Edward VII (1841-1910)** of England.

In 1904, Marconi entered into an agreement with the Cunard steamship line to create the first ship-to-shore communications system. This system proved to be a vital factor in saving lives in the event of maritime disasters, such as the sinking of the Titanic in 1912. The Titanic incident made Marconi a worldwide celebrity and insured his success and that of wireless communication technology.

During **World War I (1914-1918),** Marconi was in charge of wireless communications for Italian military forces, and after the war, he converted his yacht, *Electra,* to a floating laboratory from which he conducted further experiments in communications.

Possibly the most brilliant physicist and mathematician to ever live, and certainly the greatest since **Sir Isaac Newton** (see page 52), **Albert Einstein** was born near Ulm, Germany, on March 14, 1879, but his family moved to Italy when he was 15. Although he did not talk until age three and experienced trouble in school as a child, he received his doctorate from Zurich (Switzerland) Polytechnic in 1900 and became a teacher. He later worked at the Swiss patent office and wrote papers on theoretical physics in his spare time.

In 1905, he began publishing the components of his **General Theory of Relativity** in which he demonstrated that time was relative to the speed at which the observer was traveling. He also theorized that the speed light travels, which we understand as 186,000 miles per second, is not absolute.

The essence of Einstein's General Theory of Relativity states that if matter is converted into energy, then energy released can be shown in the seemingly simple formula $E = mc^2$, where c represents the velocity of light, E represents energy and m represents mass. This formula demonstrates that a small mass can be converted into a huge amount of energy, and it shows mathematically a means of developing nuclear weapons and reactors for the production of nuclear energy. Einstein's discoveries about nuclear energy also explained the nature of stars (including our own Sun) by demonstrating that if the Sun was really *on fire,* it would have been consumed years ago. In a nuclear reaction, Einstein suggested that huge quantities of light and heat could go on being created, with the loss of only a very small mass.

Einstein returned to Germany in 1914 and continued his work on **Photoelectric Effect,** studying how metals emit electrons when exposed to light, and it was for this work that he received the **1921 Nobel Prize in physics.** He also contributed to early theoretical work that led to the harnessing of **nuclear energy.**

Because he was Jewish, Einstein suffered discrimination after the Nazis came to power in Germany in 1933, so he emigrated to the United States, where he carried on his work at Princeton University. Convinced that the Germans would try to build nuclear weapons, Einstein convinced President **Franklin Roosevelt** (see page 94) that the United States should begin such a development program immediately. Although the Germans failed to produce such weapons, the Americans succeeded.

At the end of the war, Einstein continued to work on his **Unified Field Theory** which stated that all basic laws of physics could be unified in a single theory. His later work was considered so profound and complex that it remained untouched for several years after his death at Princeton, New Jersey, on April 18, 1955.

Albert Einstein.

Josef Vissarionovich Djugashvili, the man responsible for the violent deaths of more human beings than any other person in modern—and possibly all—history, was born at Gori, Georgia, on December 21, 1879, the son of a failed shoemaker who physically abused him. After his father's death in 1890, his mother forced him into a seminary, but he quit to become a member of the Social Democratic Party in 1901, and in 1903 he joined the **Bolshevik Party of Nikolai Lenin** (see page 87). In 1912, at the time Lenin made him a member of their Bolshevik Central Committee, he took the name **"Stalin,"** meaning "man of steel."

Stalin took part in the 1917 **Russian Revolution,** in which the Bolsheviks overthrew the government of Russia's **Tsar Nicholas II (1868-1918),** and he became general secretary of the Central Committee in 1922, the same year that the **Union of Soviet Socialist Republics (USSR)** was formed. This position gave him the control of the **Bolshevik**—later **Communist**—party apparatus. When Lenin died in 1924, Stalin pushed aside his various rivals, including the more radical **Leon Trotsky (1879-1940)** to seize absolute power within the party and the USSR.

Stalin's goals were to set about nationalizing all farm land, factories and other real state, and to industrialize the USSR on a mass scale. The latter goal was achieved through three **five year plans** he launched in 1928, 1933 and 1938. Refusing to tolerate any internal opposition in his ranks, he arrested, tried and executed well over half of the party's Central Committee and Party Congress. During the 1930s, he jailed and/or executed as many as 20 million people, mostly Russians.

Despite Stalin's brutality—or perhaps because of it—the USSR was totally unprepared for **World War II (1939-1945)** when Germany invaded on June 22, 1941.

Josef Stalin.

The Germans enjoyed immediate military success, and it was only the severe Russian winter that blunted their drive on Moscow in December. Stalin rallied his followers, built the world's largest army and helped the Western Allies to vanquish Germany in 1945. In the process of liberating numerous sovereign states from German possession, Stalin's Red Army occupied the previously independent states between Poland and Romania.

As World War II neared its end, Stalin, **Winston Churchill** (see page 88) and **Franklin D. Roosevelt** (see page 94) met at the **Yalta Conference** in the Soviet Crimea to discuss the configuration of postwar Europe, where Stalin convinced them to adopt his plan to permanently cripple Germany and maintain "friendly" states in Eastern Europe.

Although Stalin was a Communist, his motivation sprang not so much from a desire to perpetuate the doctrines of that economic philosophy but rather from his political concept of a powerful Soviet Union surrounded by nations that were totally under its control. He supported a Communist revolution in China that succeeded in 1949. He had contemplated using the Red Army to swallow Western Europe, but was held in check by the American nuclear arsenal and the implicit threat that an attack on Western Europe would invite American nuclear retaliation. Thus began the **Cold War.** Although Stalin died on March 5, 1953, and was later discredited by his successors, the nuclear stalemate between the United States and the USSR continued for another generation.

A controversial general who was once dubbed the "American Caesar," **Douglas MacArthur** was born in Little Rock, Arkansas, on January 26, 1880, the son of General **Arthur MacArthur,** a highly decorated **Civil War (1861-1865)** hero. He graduated from the US Military Academy (USMA) at West Point at the head of the class of 1903, and went on to serve in a number of posts, including as an aide to President **Theodore Roosevelt** (see page 83).

During **World War I (1914-1918),** MacArthur served with, and eventually became commander of, the famed 42d Infantry Division (aka Rainbow Division) in France. As superintendent of the USMA from 1919 to 1922, he instituted many far-reaching improvements. Like his father, he served in the Philippines, which had been an American Commonwealth since 1898. In 1930, he became US Army Chief of Staff, serving until his retirement in 1937. At that time, he was named field marshall for the Philippine Army.

On December 7, 1941 (December 8 in the Philippines), Japan attacked the US Navy base at Pearl Harbor in Hawaii, as well as American bases in the Philippines, bringing the United States into **World War II (1939-1945).** President **Franklin D. Roosevelt** (see page 94) recalled MacArthur to active duty to lead the defense of the Philippines.

MacArthur was forced to withdraw to Australia in March 1942, where he became **Supreme Allied Commander** for the **Southwest Pacific Theater,** charged with preventing a Japanese invasion of Australia and recapturing the territory that Japan had taken.

Despite the fact that Allied resources were primarily committed to the war in Europe, MacArthur's brilliantly conceived counteroffensive strategy succeeded at virtually every turn. During 1943 and 1944 he defeated the Japanese in New Guinea and undertook an **Island Hopping Campaign** in the Pacific. The latter strategy involved capturing only *some* of the enemy's island bases, leaving others isolated because the Allies controlled the seas. MacArthur returned to the Philippines in October 1944, and by August 1945, the Allies, under his Supreme Command, had reached the threshold of Japan itself. On September 3, he accepted the unconditional Japanese surrender.

After the war, MacArthur became the de facto ruler of Japan. He introduced a modern democratic constitution and made major reforms in the country's feudalistic social structure.

When North Korea invaded South Korea on June 25, 1950, touching off the **Korean War (1950-1953),** the **United Nations (UN)** called upon the United States to organize a military defense of the South. Named UN Commander, MacArthur sent the handful of troops he had available in Japan, but they were barely able to maintain a foothold in Korea. Given additional troops, he cleverly outflanked the North Koreans in September with an amphibious invasion at **Inchon** deep behind their lines.

North Korea had all but been defeated when the Chinese intervened in November with a force vastly superior in size. MacArthur advocated attacking their bases within China, but this tactic was rejected by American officials who favored a containment strategy rather than victory, and MacArthur was relieved of his command by President **Harry Truman (1884-1972)** in April 1951.

MacArthur considered a political career but instead went into retirement and wrote his memoirs, *Reminiscences* (1964). He died on April 5, 1964.

Remembered by many in the art world as the greatest artist of the twentieth century, **Pablo Picasso** was a man of minimal artistic talent, but whose genius for self-promotion made him a legend in his own time, as well as a very wealthy man. He also benefitted from the belief that emerged in the mid-twentieth century that visual arts had value only if interpreted as such by a member of a small coterie of elite art critics.

Picasso was born on October 25, 1881, in Malaga, Spain, the son of an art teacher. He attended the Academy of Fine Arts in Barcelona in 1895 and experimented with a variety of artistic styles that were current at the turn of the century. While living in Paris, he was influenced by **Paul Cezanne (1839-1906)** during his **Blue Period (1901-1904).** Picasso then entered his **Rose Period,** during which time he painted clowns and circus performers in a lighter, more decorative style.

Pablo Picasso.

Beginning in 1907, Picasso and **Georges Braque (1882-1963)** innovated a crude, simplistic style based on primitive art which involved the rendering of three-dimensional objects on exaggeratedly flat planes, a style they called **Cubism.** Picasso also experimented with **collage,** a craft form often enjoyed by children that for Picasso meant gluing actual objects, as well as cloth and printed papers, to the surface of his paintings. Although Picasso never abandoned the use of Cubism, during the 1920s he also incorporated some elements of the dreamlike and then-fashionable style of **Surrealism** into his work.

Perhaps Picasso's single most important work was a giant mural entitled *Guernica,* which he executed in 1937. Measuring 11.5' x 25.7' (3.5 x 7.8 meters), it is a moving tribute to the people who died in an attack on the city of the same name during the **Spanish Civil War (1936-1939).**

Having lived in Paris from the turn of the century to the end of World War II, Picasso moved to southern France in the late 1940s, where he remained for the rest of his life. During this time, he devoted his time not to exploring new styles of art but to capitalizing on his own success by creating numerous editions of prints. His timing proved to be perfect, as the 1950s witnessed the beginning of a trend toward viewing living visual artists as important marketable commodities. Paintings by old masters had long been prized, but the world of art dealers, which became centered in New York City during World War II, realized the immense value of promoting and capitalizing on artists that were still alive to sign their works. Prints offered a means to maximize the number of signed works, and Picasso was a pioneer in this field. He died in France on April 8, 1973, having exploited his fame and his name like no other artist before him.

86. FRANKLIN DELANO ROOSEVELT
1882-1945

The only man ever elected to a third or fourth term as president of the United States, **Franklin Delano Roosevelt** was born in Hyde Park, New York, on January 30, 1882, the son of **James Roosevelt** and **Sarah Delano Roosevelt,** both members of wealthy, old line, Anglo-Dutch-American families. President **Theodore Roosevelt** (see page 83) was a distant cousin. After graduating from Harvard University and Columbia University Law School, he began practicing law in 1907. He married his cousin **Anna Eleanor Roosevelt (1884-1962)** in 1905 and entered politics in 1911. He served as a New York state senator, Assistant Secretary of the Navy under President **Woodrow Wilson (1856-1924),** and in 1920 ran unsuccessfully as the Democratic Party's vice-presidential candidate.

After he contracted **polio** in 1921, Roosevelt's legs remained crippled for the rest of his life. He overcame the effects of his disability, learned to walk using crutches and leg braces and re-entered politics in 1924. He was elected governor of New York in 1928 and ran for president of the United States in 1932 promising a bold, new plan of action to rescue the nation from the effects of the **Great Depression,** the worst economic disaster of the twentieth century. He campaigned against the incumbent president, **Herbert Clark Hoover (1874-1964),** proposing nothing less than the most "activist" government in American history and convincing people that they "had nothing to fear but fear itself."

Elected by a landslide, Roosevelt took office in March 1933 and succeeded in pushing his innovative economic plan, which he called the **New Deal,** through Congress in just 100 days. The Legislature gave Roosevelt an unprecedented $3.3 billion to spend on the creation of new jobs

Franklin Delano Roosevelt.

and passed the **National Industrial Recovery Act (NRA),** which gave the president the power to control the economy.

Roosevelt hoped that the NRA would spur private sector economic growth, but instead it came under heavy criticism from business leaders, and in 1936 it was ruled unconstitutional. Undaunted, Roosevelt continued to propose numerous innovative—albeit controversial—New Deal programs such as the **Tennessee Valley Authority (TVA),** which built a series of hydroelectric dams on the Tennessee River to generate electricity and jobs in one of the most economically depressed regions of the country, and the **Works Progress Administration (WPA),** which put thousands of people to work on public works projects ranging from building bridges to writing travel guides.

In 1935, Congress passed the landmark **Social Security Act,** a nationally enforced savings retirement plan that would prove to be one of Roosevelt's most lasting lega-

cies. Despite continuing controversy surrounding his programs, Roosevelt won re-election by another landslide in 1936 and went on to win third and fourth terms in 1940 and 1944.

When **World War II (1939-1945)** began, the United States remained apart from the hostilities while continuing to give moral support to Britain. Roosevelt was well aware of the probability that the United States would eventually be drawn into the war. As they had in **World War I (1914-1918),** German submarines had begun attacking American ships in the Atlantic. Roosevelt met secretly with British Prime Minister **Winston Churchill** (see page 88) in August 1941, and the two leaders agreed to work together if the United States was forced into the war.

On December 7, 1941, bombers launched from Japanese aircraft carriers struck at American military installations in Hawaii, particularly the Pearl Harbor Naval Base. The attack was a complete surprise and an immense success. When it ended, 3000 Americans were dead, 100 aircraft had been destroyed and the US Navy's Pacific Fleet had been decimated.

Eight out of the nine battleships that had been anchored in Pearl Harbor had been put out of commission. The following day, President Roosevelt, calling December 7 "a day of infamy," asked Congress for a declaration of war. On December 11, Germany and Italy declared war against the United States and Japan declared war on Britain.

Roosevelt then assembled a management team of incredible intellect and genius who planned not only for military victory but for the overwhelming industrial support—it was called the **Arsenal of Democracy**—that would make victory not only possible, but *inevitable*. The unbelievably awesome military-industrial complex that Roosevelt and his team created, virtually overnight, was unprecedented and unequalled in human history, and will almost certainly never occur again.

When Roosevelt died on April 12, 1945, the war was not over, but victory was in sight. He was less than a year into his fourth term, but he served longer than any American president before, or since, and he left a legacy of social and economic reform that still remains.

Roosevelt confers with Winston Churchill during World War II.

Charles Spencer "Charlie" Chaplin, the man who first defined motion picture comedy, was born in London, England, on April 16, 1889, the son of impoverished music hall performers. He followed in his parents' footsteps, becoming a professional clown at the age of 17. In 1912, he emigrated to the United States, where the film industry was still in its infancy.

Chaplin was hired by **Mack Sennett,** whose **Keystone Studios** had become famous for its slapstick comedies, and he completed 35 short films for Sennett. He created the character of the **Little Tramp,** which was an immediate hit with audiences and was destined to become one of the most endearing and enduring images in twentieth century popular culture.

Charles Chaplin.

Even as his fame as a performer continued to grow, Chaplin turned to directing. In 1919, in conjunction with **Mary Pickford, Douglas Fairbanks** and **D.W. Griffith,** he founded **United Artists Studios.** After filming dozens of short films, Chaplin appeared as the Little Tramp in three major full-length motion pictures. *The Gold Rush* (1925), *City Lights* (1931) and *Modern Times* (1936) were tremendous commercial successes and solidified his reputation.

Chaplin's first "talkie" (motion picture with sound), and his first major role as a character other than the Little Tramp, was the film *The Great Dictator* (1940), in which he parodied **Adolf Hitler** (see page 97). During the 1940s, he was criticized for his four marriages to women much younger than himself, for having a child out of wedlock and for his Communist leanings. In 1943, the 54-year-old actor married his fourth, and last, wife, **Oona O'Neill,** the 18-year-old daughter of playwright **Eugene O'Neill (1888-1953).** Their daughter, **Geraldine Chaplin (b. 1944)** had a small part in her father's last major film, *Limelight* (1952), in which he both produced and starred. Geraldine went on to become a respected star in her own right a quarter century later.

Also in 1952, Chaplin, who had retained his British citizenship, was threatened with deportation from the United States if he did not renounce his alleged Communist sympathies. Enraged, Chaplin went into self-imposed exile in Switzerland, where he remained for 20 years. He returned to the United States in 1972 to accept an **Academy Award** for Special Achievement from the **Motion Picture Academy of America,** and in 1975, he was knighted by **Queen Elizabeth II (b. 1926)** of England. He died on Christmas Day 1977. In 1978, his body was stolen from the cemetery and has never been recovered.

Adolf Hitler, the man who many now regard as history's most infamous villain, was born on April 20, 1889, the son of Alois Hitler, a customs inspector at Braunau, Austria. Eager to become an artist, Hitler applied to the Academy of Fine Arts in Vienna in 1907 and 1908 but was refused. He spent his spare time with occultists and political extremists from both ends of the political spectrum who influenced his intellectual development and reinforced his hatred of the middle class, especially people of Jewish descent.

When World War I (1914-1918) started in 1914, Hitler was rejected by the Austrian army but accepted by the German army. He won the Iron Cross for bravery, but after the war he—like many others—found himself unable to get a job. Postwar Germany was in upheaval. The collapse of the monarchy and the economy provided fertile ground for the growth of extremist philosophies, ranging from communism to nationalism. Hitler traveled to Munich, where he became an early member of the National Socialist German Workers' Party (NSDAP)—Nazi for short.

The global economic depression that began in 1929 made it possible for the NSDAP to make political inroads with the disgruntled German electorate. Gradually, the Nazis became recognized as a legitimate political party and Hitler, who was a brilliant orator, began to garner wide support. By 1933, the Nazi Party was so powerful that President Paul von Hindenberg (1847-1934) was compelled to appoint Hitler as Germany's chancellor. Hitler promptly began to use his new position as a power base to oust Hindenberg and seize dictatorial control. He set about to rearm the German military and reassert German territorial interests in Europe.

In March 1938, Hitler annexed Austria, making it part of Germany, and in March 1939 his troops took control of Czechoslovakia. Although Britain and France complained loudly, in the interest of avoiding a war, they took no action. On August 24, 1939, Germany signed a nonaggression pact with the Soviet Union, and on September 1, the German army launched a full-scale attack on Poland. On September 3, Britain and France declared that a state of war had existed for two days. World War II (1939-1945) had begun.

The first two years of the war were marked by outstanding military successes for German forces. France fell in a matter of weeks in 1940 and, although England was never invaded, its military power in Europe was totally negated. Hitler's total domination of Europe lasted from 1941 to 1944, when the Anglo-American Allies seized major footholds in France and Italy and the Soviet armies forced the Germans to retreat back across eastern Europe. By early 1945, Germans were desperately defending their own soil, and by May 7, the war was over.

Hitler's mood in 1939-1942 had been one of invincible optimism. He made plans for a German empire, or Reich (rīk) in Europe that would last 1000 years. To fulfill his dream of a racially pure Reich, he set up a network of crematoria for the mass execution of Jews, gypsies and others he considered "undesirable." Between 1943 and 1945, Hitler grew increasingly depressed and angry, and became involved with occult beliefs in which a form of black magic, combined with mysterious secret weapons, would save Germany from defeat. On April 30, 1945, as Soviet armies encircled Berlin, Germany's capital, evidence indicates that Hitler, who had hidden in a fortified underground bunker, murdered his long-time mistress Eva Braun, whom he had just married, and then took his own life.

The most monumental figure in French political life since **Napoleon Bonaparte** (see page 62), **Charles Andre Marie Joseph de Gaulle** was born in Lille in northern France on November 22, 1890 and entered the French military academy at St. Cyr in 1910. He graduated a few weeks before the start of **World War I (1914-1918),** during which he served in combat as a lieutenant in the French army. After the war, he served in the military occupation of Germany and in France's overseas colonies before returning to France to accept an appointment to the Supreme War Council and the Council of the National Defense.

In the 1930s, French defensive strategy—that is, defense against neighboring Germany, its traditional foe—relied on the idea of a heavily fortified, but fixed, defensive perimeter known as the **Maginot Line.** De Gaulle drew the ire of his military superiors by criticizing the Maginot Line and the concept of a fixed defense. Instead, he advocated a mobile force of tanks and armored vehicles, such as the Germans were then developing. After **World War II (1939-1945)** began on September 1, 1939, the Germans initially made no attempt to attack the Maginot Line. However, in May 1940, German forces moved against France, circling to the north of the Maginot Line. De Gaulle led several successful actions with the few tanks he had, but overall, the French were caught unprepared, and by June 14, the Germans had captured Paris and defeated France.

De Gaulle escaped to Britain, where he broadcast an appeal to the French people to continue the resistance. The French **Vichy** government, installed under the auspices of German occupation troops, condemned de Gaulle, but with British (and later American) support, he proceeded to assemble his **Free French Army.** On June 6, 1944,

when the Allies landed in Normandy to liberate France and Europe, de Gaulle and his army were present, and he led them triumphantly into Paris 10 weeks later. He then formed a provisional French government with himself as president, but he retired in 1946.

In 1958, when the war in the French colony of Algeria threatened to ignite a civil war in France itself, de Gaulle came out of retirement and was elected president by an overwhelming majority. He resolved the Algerian problem by granting them independence and then turned to rebuilding the fabric of French economic and political life. Under his **Fourth Republic,** France reclaimed its role as one of the dominant political powers in European—and world—affairs.

In 1968, however, a student-worker revolt weakened confidence in de Gaulle's government, and on April 28, 1969, he resigned, turning the Fourth Republic over to **Georges Pompidou (1911-1974).** De Gaulle died at Colombey les Deux Eglises on November 9, 1970.

Charles de Gaulle.

Born in Denison, Texas, on October 14, 1890, **Dwight David Eisenhower** rose from a childhood of poverty to serve as Supreme Commander of Allied Forces in Europe during **World War II (1939-1945)** and as President of the United States for two terms between 1952-1960. He graduated from the United States Military Academy at West Point in the Class of 1915, a legendary class which contained more men who later became high-ranking generals than any other.

Eisenhower's career in the US Army, during which he served both at home and abroad, spanned a quarter century and culminated in his promotion to commander of the US Third Army. After Japan attacked Pearl Harbor on December 7, 1941, and the United States entered World War II, General Eisenhower was assigned to the staff of Chief of Staff General **George Catlett Marshall (1880-1959)**. In June 1942, he was given command of the growing number of troops in the **European Theater**. In 1943, he was named Supreme Commander of all Allied Forces (American, British, Canadian, French, etc.) which would take part in a concerted effort to retake occupied Europe from the Germans.

Thus, Eisenhower came to command the largest military operation of the entire war—the **Allied Invasion of Normandy (Operation Overlord)** in northern France on June 6, 1944. Under his leadership, 2.9 million Allied troops, 5000 ships and over 15,000 aircraft took part in crossing the English Channel from England to land on the Normandy coast. The landings were a success, and by August 25, the Allies marched triumphantly into Paris. The Anglo-American Allies brought the war home to Germany early in 1945, reaching the banks of the Rhine River by March 8. On May 7, which was designated **Victory in Europe (VE) Day,** Eisenhower met

Dwight D. Eisenhower.

with Germany's top military leaders in Rheims, France, as they formally accepted Allied terms for unconditional surrender.

After the war, Eisenhower served as US Army Chief of Staff, as president of Columbia University and as commander of the **North Atlantic Treaty Organization (NATO)**. In 1952, he accepted the Republican nomination for President of the United States, was elected and became a popular president during his two terms in office. Domestically, he launched the construction of the **St. Lawrence Seaway** and the **Interstate Highway System**. In foreign affairs, he ended the **Korean War (1950-1953)** and established a network of military alliances around the world, but refused to commit military forces to the civil war heating up in Vietnam. Despite his efforts to the contrary, relations with the Soviet Union declined into a state of **Cold War,** a perpetual military stand-off.

Prevented from running for a third term by the **Twenty-second Amendment** to the United States Constitution, Eisenhower retired to his farm in Gettysburg, Pennsylvania, in 1961, where he wrote several books. He died on March 28, 1969.

Mao Tse-Tung, the first man to unite China politically in modern times, was born into a peasant family on December 26, 1893 at Shao-shan in the Hunan Province at a time when China was ruled by the **Ch'ing (Manchu) Dynasty** but dominated by foreign powers. When the Ch'ing Dynasty collapsed in 1912, the **Kuomintang** (Koo'mĭn-təng) (Nationalist) Party was declared a republic, and **Dr. Sun Yat-sen (1866-1922)** became president. The new Chinese Republic purged most of the foreign enclaves in the country, but unfortunately they were simply replaced by others ruled by Chinese warlords.

Mao Tse-Tung.

Young Mao served briefly in the Nationalist Army, and in 1918 he went to Peking to study. Being poor, he could not afford to attend school full-time and he developed an intense hatred for intellectuals and the middle class. In 1921, he was one of the founders of the **Chinese Communist Party,** and in 1927 he returned to Hunan to organize peasant support. Meanwhile, **General Chiang Kai-shek (1887-1975)** succeeded Sun Yat-sen in 1927, not only facing opposition from the warlords but a major Japanese invasion that began on July 7, 1937. Chiang soon lost much of Kuomintang-controlled China to the Japanese. When the Allies declared war against Japan in 1941, Chiang's Nationalist China allied itself with them. Although the Allies never actually drove the invading forces out of China, the Japanese withdrew as part of their unconditional surrender signed on **Victory in Japan (VJ) Day.**

During the war, Chiang had nominally allied himself with the Chinese Communist leader Mao, but after the Japanese withdrawal, Mao initiated a civil war for control of the country. Mao had built a solid power base among the peasantry, who had suffered through years of war and foreign domination.

On October 1, 1949, Chiang's Kuomintang government fled to the island of Taiwan and Mao declared the unified nation to be the **People's Republic of China.** Mao then undertook the greatest social transformation of a nation and a people in human history, eliminating all private property and bringing all land and property under state control. He then effectively sealed China off from the rest of the world. It was virtually textbook **Marxism** in which everyone worked for the state and the state was theoretically composed of "the people," although the state was actually Mao and his ruling elite. Mao's **Great Leap Forward** program ultimately failed to create the intended economic utopia he envisioned, and he responded to critics by launching a **Cultural Revolution** during which his **Red Guards** killed thousands of Mao's critics.

In 1972, in a sudden change of heart, Mao received President **Richard Nixon (b. 1913)** of the United States, a nation that had represented everything that Mao had opposed. This led, after Mao's death on September 9, 1976, to a relaxing of Marxism in China and to that country once more becoming an active member of the world's community of nations.

Remembered as perhaps the single most outstanding player in the history of the American sport of **baseball, George Herman "Babe" Ruth** was born in Baltimore, Maryland, on February 6, 1895 and began his career as a left-handed pitcher with the **Boston Red Sox** in 1914. He enjoyed an extraordinary career as a pitcher, garnering 89 victories in 158 games, a 3-0 win record in the **1914-1916 World Series,** a 2.28 earned run average (ERA) and a stretch of 29 consecutive scoreless innings. Incredibly, the Red Sox traded him to the **New York Yankees** in 1919, and it was with the Yankees that he earned the reputation that eventually placed him at the apogee in the pantheon of all-time baseball greats.

In 1919, professional baseball was in decline because of public disgust in the wake of the **"Black Sox Scandal"** in which the Chicago White Sox took payoffs to throw games. Playing for New York, the "Babe" was in the media capital of the Western Hemisphere, and his engaging manner quickly made him a favorite of New York sports writers. Because of this, he is credited with helping restore the popularity of baseball and institutionalizing it as "the national pastime."

More than just a loveable character, Ruth quickly established himself as one of the greatest batters in the history of baseball, and certainly the greatest of his era. His hitting prowess was quickly recognized by the Yankees, who moved him from the pitcher's mound to the outfield to preserve his arm. He responded with a record 54 home runs and a .376 batting average in his first season in 1919. Having earned the nickname the "Sultan of Swat," he topped his own record with 59 home runs in 1921 and 60 in 1927, with the latter record standing for the next 47 years! Ruth led the American League in home runs for 12 years through 1931 and is still one of

only two men (the other being Hank Aaron) to have earned more than 700 hits in his career.

Even today, Ruth continues to be tied for second place in the total number of runs scored (2174) in a career. He and teammate **Henry Louis "Lou" Gehrig (1903-1942)** formed a powerful hitting duo that took the Yankees to the World Series seven times between 1921 and 1932. **Yankee Stadium,** the parthenon of the pastime, became known to fans as the "house that Ruth built."

In the decade that he was in his prime, Ruth was to baseball what Mozart had been to classical music: a man who demonstrated an extraordinary, unparalleled brilliance in his chosen profession but who exercised virtually no discipline in his personal life. However, when Ruth began to fade, he faded fast during several wholly forgettable seasons with the Boston Braves before he retired in 1935. He died on August 16, 1948.

George Herman "Babe" Ruth.

A visionary engineer who masterminded the effort to put human beings on the surface of the Moon, **Wernher Magnus Maximillian von Braun** was born in Germany on March 23, 1912, and received his doctorate in physics from the University of Berlin in 1934. His avid interest in rockets led him to study the work of American rocket pioneer **Robert Goddard (1882-1945)**, who had invented the liquid-fuel rocket in 1926.

Von Braun was also an advocate of the seemingly far-fetched idea of human space travel. His work in rocketry landed him a job with the German army's Ordinance Department, and in 1937 he and his staff established an advanced rocket development center at Peenemunde on the Baltic Sea. It was here that von Braun developed a series of battlefield rockets used by the German army in **World War II (1939-1945)**. The most advanced of these was the **A-4,** known unofficially as the **V-2,** or vengeance weapon, second, that was a 47-foot (14.5-meter) supersonic missile capable of hitting targets in Britain when launched from pads in Germany. Over 5000 A-4s were launched against Britain and the Belgian city of Antwerp after it was liberated by the Allies in 1944.

After the war, von Braun was taken prisoner by the US Army, to whom he quickly offered his services. He developed the US Army's **Jupiter** and **Redstone** rockets, the latter of which was used to launch the first American Earth-orbiting satellite, **Explorer 1,** on January 31, 1958. Von Braun also authored several technical books on space travel including *Across the Space Frontier* (1952) and *Conquest of the Moon* (1953). In 1960, he and his scientific team were transferred to the **National Aeronautics & Space Administration (NASA)** and given the task of building a system capable of taking humans to the Moon—the most

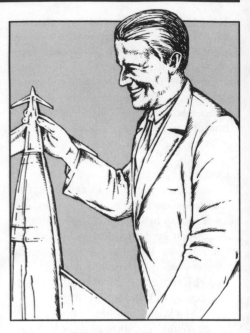

Wernher von Braun.

challenging engineering project in history. Von Braun's team designed the **Apollo** spacecraft and the huge **Saturn 5** rocket. As tall as a 34-story building and capable of 7.7 million pounds (2.9 million kg) of thrust, the Saturn 5 was the largest rocket ever built.

Between 1968 and 1972, von Braun's Saturns took nine crews of three American astronauts each to lunar orbit and back, including 12 men who actually walked on the Moon's surface.

Von Braun and his team had been an important element in NASA's plans for the landing of American astronauts on Mars, which was originally scheduled for 1981. This project was under development when it was canceled in 1969 along with NASA's master plan for human exploration of the solar system in the 1970s and 1980s. Von Braun left NASA in 1972 to join Fairchild Industries. He died on June 23, 1977.

94. JOHN FITZGERALD KENNEDY
1917-1963

The youngest man ever to be elected President of the United States, **John "Jack" Fitzgerald Kennedy** was born in Brookline, Massachusetts on May 29, 1917, the second son of **Joseph P. Kennedy** and **Rose Fitzgerald,** both descendants of prominent Massachusetts Irish-Catholic families. The elder Kennedy, one of the richest men in America, was a tough businessman who had served as ambassador to Britain. Jack Kennedy graduated from Harvard University in 1940 and served in the US Navy in **World War II (1939-1945),** where he became a decorated war hero. He entered politics after the war, served three terms in Congress and was elected to the US Senate in 1952. He married socialite **Jacqueline Bouvier (b. 1929)** in 1953, and in 1957 his book, *Profiles in Courage,* won a **Pulitzer Prize.**

After winning the Democratic Party's presidential nomination in 1960, Kennedy was elected president by a narrow margin. He took office in 1961 with a promise that he would provide a vigorous new vision of America's position in the world. The most serious crises that his administration subsequently faced sprang from the festering **Cold War** between the United States and the Soviet Union that dated from the end of World War II. Premier **Nikita Khrushchev** (Kroosh-chĕf′) **(1894-1971)** decided to take advantage of Kennedy's preoccupation with his domestic agenda to consolidate the Soviet position around the world. In 1961, he ordered construction of a concrete wall through the center of the city of Berlin, closing the border between East and West Germany. The **Berlin Wall** was seen as a tangible manifestation of the political realities of the Cold War. In **Cuba,** Soviet-backed Communist leader **Fidel Castro (b. 1927)** thwarted a United States-sponsored invasion at the **Bay of Pigs,** making the United States appear inept.

In September 1962, Khrushchev told Kennedy that any further attacks on Cuba would be considered an *act of war.* Soon after, it was discovered that the Soviets had been positioning missiles with nuclear warheads in Cuba. On October 22, Kennedy publicly demanded that Khrushchev withdraw the missiles or the United States would attack Cuba. A flurry of negotiations ensued as both sides prepared for war. American warships surrounded Cuba to enforce a "quarantine" on all shipping, and the United States prepared to attack if necessary. Finally, on October 28, Khrushchev told Kennedy that he would remove all missiles if the United States promised not to invade Cuba. The **Cuban Missile Crisis** was the hottest moment in the Cold War, but a nuclear cataclysm had been averted.

Kennedy emerged from this crisis as a hero and turned his attention to such things as a **Nuclear Test Ban Treaty** and to embracing the **Civil Rights Movement** led by **Dr. Martin Luther King, Jr.** (see page ••). On November 22, Kennedy was in the middle of a speech-making trip to Dallas, Texas, when he was shot and killed by at least two gunmen, one of whom is thought to be **Lee Harvey Oswald (1939-1963),** who was originally believed to have acted alone.

President Kennedy's murder was all the more shocking because it was the first assassination of a major world leader since the advent of the television and instantaneous global communications. In the United States, where the boyish, dynamic John Kennedy, noted for his gifted oratory, had fired the imagination of the postwar generation, there was a profound sense of shock and grief. For many who came of age during the 1960s, Kennedy's death proved to be a seminal occurrence in their lives.

95. DR. MARTIN LUTHER KING, JR.
1929-1968

Perhaps aside from **Mohandas Gandhi** (see page 86), no one in the twentieth century did more to advance the cause of peaceful social change than **Dr. Martin Luther King, Jr.**, an African-American Baptist Church minister. He was born in Atlanta, Georgia, on January 15, 1929, attended Crozer Theological Seminary and earned his doctorate in philosophy from Boston University in 1955. After his ordination, he became the pastor of the Exeter Avenue Baptist Church in Montgomery, Alabama in 1955, shortly before a black woman named **Rosa Parks (b. 1913)** touched off a controversy by refusing to give up her seat to a white man on one of the city's public transit buses. Dr. King helped organize a successful citywide bus boycott by black riders that attracted national attention and served to launch the American **Civil Rights Movement.**

Dr. Martin Luther King, Jr.

Despite constitutional guarantees of equal treatment regardless of race, in the 1950s Southern states still maintained local laws which curtailed the rights of black Americans. In a practice known as segregation, certain public facilities, from drinking fountains to seats on city buses, were restricted as "whites only." Private businesses, such as restaurants, had the right to exclude blacks from their establishments. Even public schools remained segregated until 1964. The Civil Rights Movement was an effort to eliminate segregation, and it sought to assert the civil rights of black people to achieve integration into society and fully guarantee that they could exercise their legal rights, such as the right to vote.

After the Montgomery bus boycott, Dr. King emerged as a major leader of the Civil Rights Movement, and over the next nine years, the movement gained both momentum and nationwide support, especially after **John F. Kennedy** (see page 103)

became president in 1961. After numerous peaceful protests, a major turning point in the movement occurred during a massive civil rights march on Washington, DC, in the summer of 1963 that culminated with Dr. King's immortal "I Have a Dream" speech on August 24. On July 2, 1964, the **Civil Rights Act** was passed outlawing all forms of discrimination in public facilities, accommodations and schools. That same year, Dr. King was awarded the Nobel Peace Prize for his work in promoting the civil rights of African-Americans.

As leader of the **Southern Christian Leadership Council (SCLC),** Dr. King energetically undertook the task of bringing black people into the mainstream of American life and improving living conditions for poor and disadvantaged Americans of all races. He was in the process of organizing another march on Washington when he was assassinated at a motel in Memphis, Tennessee, by **James Earl Ray** on April 4, 1968. In 1983, his birthday was made a national holiday.

96. MIKHAIL GORBACHEV
b. 1931

Mikhail Sergeyevich Gorbachev, the Soviet leader who paved the way for the collapse of the **Union of Soviet Socialist Republics (USSR)** and the dominance of the **Communist Party of the Soviet Union (CPSU)** in Russia, was born on March 2, 1931, at Privolnoye, Russia. He studied law at Moscow State University and then worked as a machine operator at Stavropol before becoming active in regional CPSU activities in 1955.

Gorbachev worked his way up the CPSU hierarchy, becoming a member of the Russian Supreme Soviet in 1979. In March 1985, upon the death of **Konstantin Chernenko,** he assumed the office of general secretary of the CPSU and became the most politically powerful man in the USSR. In 1990, he became executive president of the USSR, the only man to hold this post which was created to divorce the CPSU leadership role from that of the USSR.

When he assumed office, Gorbachev inherited a nation exhausted from 70 years of a failed state-controlled economy, 40 years of political **Cold War** with the West and a decade of bloody, fruitless warfare in Afghanistan. The first true political visionary to come to power in the USSR in over half a century, his vision was that of progress and reform. He promised **glasnost** (openness) and **perestroika** (restructuring) of the Soviet Union. However, the Communist state had already begun to crumble, and only the iron bands of totalitarianism held the pieces in place. As Gorbachev loosened them, pieces began to fall away. The 15 "republics" that comprised the USSR each clamored for more autonomy, and the Baltic republics of Estonia, Latvia and Lithuania sought complete independence. **Boris Yeltsin (b. 1931),** who was elected president of the vast Russian Republic in June 1991, demanded more au-tonomy for his republic, which formed the heart of the USSR.

On August 19, 1991, a group of Communist hard-liners arrested Gorbachev and declared a return to a Brezhnev-style state. To their surprise, Yeltsin stood up to them, and their coup failed within a few days. Although Yeltsin had succeeded in rescuing Gorbachev, it was clear to everyone that the governing structure of the Soviet Union had completely dissolved.

Gorbachev tried for several months to keep them together, but the Soviet Communist Party and the USSR were collapsing under their own weight. Effective on the first day of 1992, the Soviet Union and the Soviet Communist Party officially ceased to exist, and Gorbachev retired from public office to manage his **International Foundation for Social & Economic & Political Research.**

Mikhail Gorbachev.

The most brilliant physicist since **Albert Einstein** (see page 90) and possibly since **Sir Isaac Newton** (see page 52), **Stephen William Hawking** was born in England on January 8, 1942, the son of Dr. F. Hawking. He attended University College, Oxford, and Trinity Hall, Cambridge, earning his doctorate in physics in 1966. He began his career as a research assistant in the Department of Applied Mathematics at Cambridge in 1973, served as a professor from 1977 to 1979 and as Lucasian Professor of Mathematics since that time. He was also a member of the Institute of Theoretical Astronomy from 1968 to 1972.

Among Hawking's many awards have been the William Hopkins Prize of the Cambridge Philosophical Society (1976), the Maxwell Medal of the Institute of Physics (1976), the Albert Einstein Award (1978), the Gold Medal of the Royal Astronomical Society (1985), the Wolf Prize (1988), the *Sunday Times* Special Award for Literature (1989) and the Britannica Award (1989).

Stephen William Hawking.

Throughout his career, Hawking's work has been directed at linking the two major theoretical components of modern physics: quantum mechanics and Einstein's **General Theory of Relativity.** He developed the **Inflationary Theory,** which suggests the existence of multiple universes linked by **wormholes**—small, quantum fluctuations in the space-time continuum.

Among Hawking's written works that have earned him the respect of his colleagues in the field of theoretical physics have been *The Large Scale Structure of Space-Time* (with G.F.R. Ellis, 1973), *General Relativity: An Einstein Centenary Survey* (1979), *Superspace and Supergravity* (1981), *The Very Early Universe* (1983) and *300 Years of Gravitation* (1987). His 1988 book, *A Brief History of Time,* and his 1993 book, *Black Holes and Baby Universes,* both nontechnical discussions of his theories and quantum physics in general, were best-sellers and made him known to the general public.

In 1963, Hawking was diagnosed with **amyotrophic lateral sclerosis (ALS),** a degenerative nervous system disorder—commonly known as **Lou Gehrig's Disease**—which destroys muscle control while leaving mental faculties intact. Over the ensuing years, even as he proceeded with his scientific work, his body continued to deteriorate. Gradually, he lost the use of his limbs and eventually the ability to speak. By the 1980s, when his work had gained international recognition, Hawking was confined to a wheelchair and forced to speak by means of a voice synthesizer.

In the 1990s, Hawking courageously continued to work, making himself understood through the use of a computer. Capable of only minimal finger motions, the body housing one of the world's most brilliant theoretical minds was barely able to tap out ten words a minute.

Computers, or "electronic brains" evolved out of the high-speed manual calculating machines of the 1930s and 1940s. The first computers built were the **American IBM Mark 7** (1937) and the **British Colossus** (1941). Computer development continued after World War II, and the first commercial models were introduced in the 1950s. Although they were used in businesses in the 1960s, computers were huge, cumbersome and very expensive. By the 1970s, transistors began to replace vacuum tubes, and computer technology became much more accessible.

In the 1980s, computers became commonplace and changed the face of modern Western civilization with their vast capabilities to aid people with a multitude of tasks.

The idea of a personal computer in every home was born in the Santa Clara Valley south of San Francisco, California, an area which eventually become known to the world as **Silicon Valley** because of its proliferation of computer-related industries. In 1976, **Stephen Wozniak** and **Steven Paul Jobs** created a homemade microprocessor computer board called **Apple I** in Jobs's parents' garage, and the two men began to manufacture and market the Apple I to local hobbyists and electronics enthusiasts. Early in 1977, Jobs and Wozniak founded **Apple Computer, Inc.,** and in April of that year introduced the **Apple I,** the world's first **personal computer,** or **microcomputer.**

Prior to this time, computers were not only vast in size and quite expensive, but they also required specially trained operators who understood their special codes, known as "languages." Thus, computers were quite intimidating to most people. Apple's philosophy—as indicated even by its whimsical company name—was to produce computer systems that were **user**

Stephen Wozniak and Steven Jobs.

friendly, meaning that were designed to be easy to use—literally *friendly* to the users and their pocketbooks as well.

Personal computers were an immediate hit with consumers, and Apple shipped tens of thousands of these inexpensive computers worldwide. The idea of a home computer became a reality. Businesses and educational institutions that would never have been able to buy computers—or train people to use the complex computer languages—were now able to take advantage of the new technology.

Apple grew to a $500 million company in only five years, and a $5 billion company by 1989. Apple continued to dominate the industry until the giant IBM Corporation introduced its **Personal Computer (PC)** in August 1981. However, in 1984, Apple introduced the revolutionary **MacIntosh (Mac)** system, and once again became one of the leading computer companies in the world. Eventually, both Jobs and Wozniak left Apple, with Jobs going on to found another computer company in 1985.

By the 1990s, Apple and IBM divided the personal computer market, and microcomputers—thanks to the pioneering work of Jobs and Wozniak—had become a familiar fixture in businesses, schools and homes throughout the industrialized world.

Perhaps the most successful entrepreneur born in the twentieth century, **William Henry "Bill" Gates** was born in Seattle, Washington, on October 28, 1955, and first began programming computers at the age of 13. During his freshman year at Harvard University, Gates and his friend **Paul Allen** became the first people to adapt a computer language—BASIC—for microcomputers, specifically the MITS Altair computer.

In 1975, Gates dropped out of Harvard, and he and Allen moved to Albuquerque, New Mexico, where MITS was headquartered, and founded the **Microsoft Corporation.** When MITS folded in 1979, Gates and Allen returned to the Seattle area to develop **software.** The personal computer revolution had just begun and a great deal of hardware was coming on the market. Gates reasoned that the hardware coming on line would be useful to the myriad of consumers only if they had the software that would make them easy to use.

In 1980, Microsoft was chosen by **International Business Machines (IBM)** to develop the operating system for its new **Personal Computer (PC).** Microsoft bought an operating system from a programmer named **Tim Paterson** and adapted it as the **Microsoft Disk Operating System (MS-DOS)**—a textbook case of being in the right place at the right time with just the right product. During the next 10 years, millions of IBM PCs, each requiring MS-DOS, were sold worldwide. Allen retired from Microsoft in 1983 for health reasons, and Gates continued to chart the course of the company, developing a whole range of business application and recreational software, as well as operating systems, for the IBM and other computers.

By 1984, Microsoft was doing $100 million worth of business annually, and this amount doubled in 1986 when the compa-

William Henry Gates.

ny's stock was first publicly traded on the New York Stock Exchange. By 1987, with 45 percent of Microsoft stock, the boy who had dropped out of college his freshman year became the computer industry's first billionaire. Within three years, Gates's net worth surpassed two billion, and by 1994 Microsoft's net revenues were nearly $4 billion.

In the 1990s, Gates began focusing on **graphic user interface systems (GUI)** such as the well-known **Microsoft Windows** program, and on interactive, multimedia systems, such as **Compact Disk Read Only Memory (CD-ROM),** system that allows users to actively access and manipulate large volumes of information stored on compact disks.

TRIVIA QUIZ & GAMES

1. What did Nicholas Copernicus do to get in trouble with the Catholic Church? (see page 44)
2. What American president was elected to more terms of office than any other? (see page 94)
3. Most people think that Julius Caesar was a Roman emperor, but he was not. What was he really, and why do people often make this mistake? (see page 27)
4. What simple tool became the symbol of the independence movement in twentieth century India and why? (see page 86)
5. What father and son were the only non-royal rulers of England in the past 1200 years (see page 51)
6. Who was the youngest man to ever *become* president of the United States? (see page 83) Who was the youngest man to ever be *elected* president of the United States? (see page 103)
7. Who is the biggest selling poet and playwright in the world today? (see page 50)
8. Many people become famous under a name other than the one with which they were born. What were the original names of these men?
   A. Caesar Augustus (see page 28)
   B. St. Paul (see page 30)
   C. Genghis Khan (see page 37)
   D. Voltaire (see page 54)
   E. Sitting Bull (see page 76)
   F. Mark Twain (see page 77)
   G. Nikolai Lenin (see page 87)
   H. Babe Ruth (see page 101)
9. What German scientist invented a weapon that eventually led to the design of the spacecraft which landed people on the surface of the Moon? (see page 102)
10. Who was the most heinous mass murderer in world history? (see page 91)
11. What visionary French author is credited with having invented science fiction? (see page 75)
12. Who was Queen Victoria's "favorite prime minister?" (see page 67)
13. What two twentieth century leaders advocated the use of nonviolent political protest as a means to achieve social change? (see pages 86 and 104)
14. What son of a pagan and a saint later became renowned as a great Christian scholar? (see page 32)
15. Who was the first European to explore the coast of Antarctica? (see page 57)
16. Who conceived the idea of gravity while watching apples fall from a tree? (see page 52)
17. National origins can be deceiving and not all well-known leaders were born in the countries where they later became famous.
    A. What great French emperor of Italian heritage was actually born on the island of Corsica? (see page 62)
    B. What Austrian-born would-be artist believed that he was destined to lead Germany to the apex of its political glory? (see page 97)
18. What ingenious machine is named after the great mathematician Archimedes? (see page 25)
19. If Johann Gutenberg did not really invent movable type printing, why was his invention so revolutionary? (see page 40)
20. Who built the Great Wall of China and why was it constructed? (see page 26)

INDEX

Achilles 11
Actium 28
Adams, John 59
Adler, Alfred 82
Adrian I 34
Agamemnon 11
Airplane (invention of) 85
Alexander The Great 7, 22, 23, 27,
Alexander III 87
Alexandria 23, 25
Alighieri, Danté 38
St. Ambrose 32
Amraphel 9
Anne of Cleves 48
Antarctica 57
Antony, Marcus 28
Antony & Cleopatra 50
Apollo spacecraft 102
Apology (Plato's) 19, 21
Apple Computer 107
Aquinas, St. Thomas 21, 22, 38,
Archimedes 7, 25
Aristotle 19, 21-23
Arouet, François Marie *see* Voltaire
Around the World in Eighty Days 75
As You Like It 50
Asoka 24
Aspasia 17
Astronomy 22, 25, 44, 49, 52,
Athens 17-23
St. Augustine 32
Augustus (see Caesar)
Australia 57, 69
Austria 56, 60-63, 68, 74, 82, 97
Automobile 84
Averroes 22
Babylonia 9
Bach, Johann Sebastian (and family)
    53
Bacon, Sir Francis
Barnabus 30
Baseball 101
Beagle 69
Beethoven, Ludwig von 61
Bell, Alexander Graham (and family)
    78, 80
Bell Telephone Co. 80
Berengar 35
Bi Zheng 40
Bible, The (Judeo-Christian Scrip-
    tures) 9, 10, 14, 29, 30, 40
Bismarck, Otto von 74
Blucher, Gebhart von 63
Boer War 88
Boleyn, Anne 48
Bolivia 65
Bolívar, Simón 65

Bolsheviks (*see also* Communism)
    87, 91
Bonaparte, Napoleon 7, 36, 61-65,
    68, 74, 98
Booth, John Wilkes 71
Brandenberg Concertos 53
Brazil 68
Brief History of Time, A 106
Britain and British Empire (*see also*
    England) 57-59, 62, 63, 65-67,
    69, 72, 73, 82, 86, 88, 95-99,
    106
Brutus, Marcus Junius 27, 28
Buchanan, James 66
Buddha 7, 13
Bull Run 71
Buonarroti, Michelangelo *see*
    Michelangelo
Buxtehude, Deitrich 53
Caesar, Julius 7, 27, 28, 50
Caesar, Augustus (Octavian) 27, 28,
    30
Candide 54
Canute 36
Carthage 27
Catherine of Aragon 48
Catherine the Great 56
Catholicism (*see* also Christianity)
    47-49
Cassius, Gaius 28
*Celebrated Jumping Frog of
    Calaveras County, The* 77
Cezanne, Paul 93
Chamberlain, Neville 88
Chaplin, Charles 96
Charlemagne 34, 35
Chatelet, Emilie du 54
Charles I 51
Charles II 51
Chiang Kai-shek 100
China 12, 13, 15, 26, 37, 39, 91, 92,
    100,
Christ, Jesus 7, 29-31,
Christianity 10, 13, 22, 29-35, 43,
    47, 48,
Christmas Carol, A 73
Church of England 48
Churchill, Winston 7, 88, 91, 95
Civil Rights Movement (US) 103-104
Civil War (England) 51
Civil War (Spain) 93
Civil War (USA) 70-71, 76, 77
Clark, George Rogers 64
Clark, William 64
Cleopatra 28
Clemens, Samuel *see* Twain, Mark
Clement VII 48

Clipper of the Clouds 75
Cold War 91, 99, 103, 105
Columbia 65
Columbus, Christopher 7, 39, 41, 46,
    52, 57, 65
Comedy of Errors 50
Communism 87, 91, 100, 103, 105
Computers 106-108
Confucius 7, 15, 26
*Connecticut Yankee in King Arthur's
    Court, A* 77
Constantine 31
Constantinus, Flavius Valerius Aure-
    lius *see* Constantine
Continental Congress 55, 58, 59
Cook, Captain James 57
Copernicus, Nicholas 44, 49
Coster, Laurence 40
Cranmer, Thomas 48
Crazy Horse 76
Cromwell, Oliver 51
Cromwell, Richard 51
Crook, George 76
Crusades 37
Cuba 83, 103
Custer, George 76
Custis, Martha Dandridge 58
Cyrus 14, 16
Daguerre, Louis-Jacques 66
Daguerreotype 66
Daimler, Gottlieb 84
Dakota 76
Darius 16, 23
Darwin, Charles 69
David Copperfield 73
Da Vinci, Leonardo 7, 42, 54, 79
Declaration of Independence (US) 55,
    58, 59
De Gaulle, Charles 98
De Medici, Lorenzo 45
Del Verrochio, Andrea 42
Depression 94
Descarte, Rene 38
Descent of Man, The 69
Dialogues 19
Dickens, Charles 73
Dionysius 21
Disraeli, Benjamin 67, 72
Don Giovanni 60
Douglas, Stephen 70
Ecuador 65
Edison, Thomas Alva 78-79
Edward I (The Confessor) 36
Edward VI 48
Edwin Drood 73
Einstein, Albert 7, 90, 106
Eisenhower, Dwight David 99

Egbert 51
Egypt 3, 10, 23, 24
Electric lights (invention of) 78
Elizabeth I 48
Emancipation Proclamation 70
England 36, 43, 48, 50-52, 54-59,
    62, 63, 65-67, 69, 72, 73, 82, 86
Erasmus, Desiderius 43
Evolution, Theory of 69
Ferdinand V 41
Fillmore, Millard 81
Finn, Huckleberry 77
Ford, Henry (and family) 84
Ford Motor Co. 84
France 34, 42, 54-56, 60, 62-65, 68,
    74, 75, 76, 89, 97-99
Franco-Prussian War 68, 74
Franklin, Benjamin 55
Frederick I 56
Frederick II (The Great) 54, 56
Frederick Wilhelm I 56
Freise-Greene, William 79
French and Indian War 56, 58
Freud, Sigmund 82
From The Earth To The Moon 75
Galilei, Galileo 49
Gandhi, Mohandas Karamchand
    "Mahatma"
Garibaldi, Giuseppe 68
Gates, William 108
Gautama, Siddhartha *see* Buddha
Genghis Khan 7, 37, 39
George III 55
George II 56
George, David Lloyd 88
Germany 27, 40, 47, 53, 56, 60, 61-
    63, 74, 87, 88, 90, 91, 95, 97-
    99, 102, 103
Gettysburg 71, 99
Giaconda, Mona Lisa 42
Gladstone, William Ewart 67, 72
Globe Theatre 50
Goethe, Johann von 61
Goddard, Robert 102
Gorbachev, Mikhail 7, 105
Grant, Ulysses Simpson 71
Gravitation, Law of 52
Great Expectations 73
Greece 11, 14, 17-23, 25, 27
Grey, Elisha 80
Gutenberg, Johann 40, 43,
Hamilton. Alexander 59
Hamlet, Prince of Denmark 50
Hammurabi (and code thereof) 9
Harold II 36
Hastings 36
Hathaway, Anne 50

Hawking, Stephen 7, 106
Haydn, Franz Josef 61
Hector 11
Henry I 35
Henry V 50
Henry VII 48
Henry VIII 43, 48
Heraclides 20
Herodotus 18
Hertz, Heinrich 89
Hinduism 13
Hippocrates 20
Hippocratic Oath 20
Hitler, Adolf 7, 36, 82, 88, 96, 97
Holland *see* Netherlands
Holy Roman Empire 34, 35, 62
Homer 11
Hoover, Herbert 94
Huckleberry Finn, The Adventures of
    77
Howard, Catherine 48
Huss, John (Jan) 47
Hydrostatics 25
I Ching (Book of Changes) 15
IBM 107-108
Iliad 11
In Praise of Folly 43
India 13, 23, 24, 67, 86
Ireland 72
Isabella 41
Islam 13, 33
Issus 23
Italy 38, 39, 41, 42, 44, 45, 49, 62,
    68
James 30
James I 51
Japan 81, 83, 92, 95, 100
Jefferson, Thomas 55, 59, 64
Jobs, Steven 107
John XII 35
St. John the Baptist 29
John Paul II 49
Joseph 76
Journey To The Center Of The Earth
    75
Julius II 43, 45
Judaism 10, 13, 22, 29, 30, 33
Julius Caesar 50
Jung, Carl 82
Karma 12
Kennedy, John Fitzgerald 103
Kerensky, Alexander 87
King, Dr. Martin Luther, Jr. 103, 104
King Lear 50
Koran 33
Korea and Korean War 92, 99
Krushchev, Nikita 103

Kublai Khan 39
Kung Fu-Tsu *see* Confucius
Langley, Samuel 85
Lao Tsu (Lao Tse) 12, 15
Lee, Robert Edward 71
Lenin, Nicholai 87, 91
Leo III 34
Leo X 47
Lewis, Merriwether 64
Licinius 31
Lincoln, Abraham 70-71
Lippershey, Hans 49, 52
Little Big Horn 76
Locke, John 54
Louis XII 48
Louisiana Purchase 59, 63, 64
Lumiere, Auguste and Louis 79
Luther, Martin 47, 48
Lutherism 47, 48
MacArthur, Douglas (and family) 92
Magellan, Ferdinand 46, 57
Magic Flute, The 60
Maimonides 22
Mao Tse-Tung (Mao Zedong) 100
Marathon 16
Marconi, Guglielmo 89
Maria Theresa 56
Marriage of Figaro, The 60
Marshall, George 99
Martel, Charles 34
Mary, Mother of Jesus 29
Marx, Karl 87
Matsuhito (Meiji) 81
McKinley, William 83
Mecca 33
Medina 33
Meiji Reformation 81
Menes, Pharaoh 8
Merchant of Venice 50
Michaelangelo 45
Microsoft 108
Midsummer Night's Dream 50
Mohammed 7, 33
Mongols and Mongolia 37, 39
St. Monica 32
Montague, John 57
Morse Code 66
Morse, Samuel F.B. 66
Moses 11
Motion, Laws of 52
Motion Pictures 78-79, 96
Mozart, Wolfgang Amadeus (and
    family) 7, 60
Much Ado About Nothing 50
NASA 102
NATO 99
Napoleon <u>see</u> Bonaparte

Napoleon III 74
Neoplatonic philosophy 21
National Recovery Act (NRA) 94
National Socialism (Nazism) 97
Nero 30
Netherlands 43, 49, 60, 62
New Deal 94
New Zealand 57, 69
Newton, Sir Isaac 7, 12, 44, 52, 90, 106
Nicean Creed 31
Nicholas II 87, 91
Nicholas Nickleby 73
Nixon, Richard 100
Nobel Prize 90,
Normandy 36, 99
Nuclear energy and weapons 90, 103
Odyssey 11
Octavian 27, 28, 30
Olds, Ransom 84
Oliver Twist 73
Origin of Species, The 69
Otto I 35
Otto, Nicholas 84
Panama Canal 83
Parthenon 17
Parr, Catherine 48
St. Paul 30
Peel, Robert 67
Peloponnesian Confederacy and War 17, 21
Pepin the Short 34
Pericles 17,
Perictione 21
Perry, Matthew 81
Persia 14, 16, 23
St. Peter 30
    Basilica of 45
Philip of Macedonia 23
Philippines 46
Phonograph (invention of) 78
Picasso, Pablo 93
Pickwick Papers, The 73
Plato 19, 21, 22, 32
Poland 44, 56
Polo, Marco (and family) 39, 41, 52
Pompidou, Georges 98
Pompey 27
Poor Richard's Almanack 55
Pope, Alexander 54
Portugal 46
Prince and the Pauper, The 77
Principia (Mathematical Principles of Natural Philosophy) 52
Protestantism 47, 48
Prussia *see also* Germany 54, 56 62-63, 74

Psychology and Psychanalysis 82
Ptolemy 44
Puritans 51
Ramses II 10
Red Cloud 76
Reform Bill 67
Reformation 47, 48,
Relativity, Theory of 90, 106
Renaissance 25, 42-45
Republic 21
Revolutionary War (US) 55, 58, 59
Richard III 50
Roman Empire 27-31, 34, 68
Roman Empire, Holy 34, 35, 62
Rome 27-31, 34, 35, 68,
Romeo and Juliet 50
Roosevelt, Franklin Delano (and family) 7, 88, 90-92, 94-95
Roosevelt, Theodore (and family) 83, 89, 92, 94
Russia (*see also* Soviet Union) 62, 83, 87, 91, 105
Ruth, George "Babe" 101
Sacajawea 64
Samos 25
Salamis 16
Saul of Tarsus 30
Sawyer, Tom 77
Scholasticism 38
Science fiction 75
Scrooge, Ebenezar 73
Seven Years War 56
Seymour, Jane 48
Shakespeare, William (and family) 7, 50, 54, 73
Shih Huang Ti 26
Silicon Valley 107
Sioux 76
Sistine Chapel 45
Sitting Buffalo Bull 76
Smithsonian Institution 80, 85
Social Security 94
Socrates 17, 19, 21
South America 46, 65, 68, 69
Soviet Union (*see also* Russia) 87, 91, 97, 99, 100, 103, 105
Space exploration 102
Spain 41, 46, 65, 83, 93
Spanish American War 83
Sparta 17
Stalin, Josef 7, 87, 91
Suez Canal 67
Summa Theologica 38
Swan, Sir Joseph 78
Swift, Jonathan 54
Switzerland 90, 87
Tainter, Charles 78

Tale of Two Cities, A 73
Tao and Taoism 12
Tatankya Iyotake *see* Sitting Buffalo Bull
Telegraph (invention of) 66, 79
Telephone (invention of) 80
Temujin *see* Genghis Khan
Tennessee Valley Authority (TVA) 94
Thermopylae 16
Tiny Tim 73
Tom Sawyer, The Adventures of 77
Truman, Harry 92
Tudor, House of 48
Twain, Mark 77
Twenty Thousand Leagues Under The Sea 75
Ulianov, Vladimir Ilyich *see* Lenin
United Nations 92
United States of America 55, 58, 59, 64-66, 68, 70-71, 76-80, 83-85, 88, 90-92, 94-96, 99, 101-104, 107, 108
USSR *see* Soviet Union
Van Buren, Martin 66
Venezuela 65
Verne, Jules 75
Vicksburg 71
Victor Emmanuel 68
Victoria 66, 67, 72
Voltaire
Von Braun, Wernher Magnus Maximilian 102
Von Schiller, Johann 61
Washington, George 7, 58, 70
Waterloo 63
Wedgewood, Josiah 69
Wellesley, Arthur 63
Wellington *see* Wellesley
Wilhelm I and II 74
William the Conqueror 36, 48,
Wilson, Woodrow 83, 94
Works Progress Administration (WPA) 94
World War I 74, 83, 87, 88, 89, 92, 97-99
World War II 81, 82, 84-86, 88, 90-95, 97-100, 102, 103
Wozniak, Stephen 107
Wright, Orville and Wilbur 85
Wycliffe, John 47
Xenophon 19
Xerxes 16, 18
Yin and Yang 12
Yankees, New York 101
Yeltsin, Boris 105
Zaire 54